ACTIVE ENGLISH THROUGH MOVIES

BOHEMIAN RHAPSODY

THE INTERN

MONEYBALL

KAYOKO SHIOMI   **MATTHEW COOMBER**   **KANAKO MIYABAYASHI**

KINSEIDO

Kinseido Publishing Co., Ltd.

3-21 Kanda Jimbo-cho, Chiyoda-ku,
Tokyo 101-0051, Japan

First published 2021 by Kinseido Publishing Co., Ltd.

Design Nampoosha Co., Ltd.

🎧 音声ファイル無料ダウンロード

https://www.kinsei-do.co.jp/download/4125

この教科書で 🎧 DL 00 の表示がある箇所の音声は、上記 URL または QR コードにて無料でダウンロードできます。自習用音声としてご活用ください。

- ▶ PC からのダウンロードをお勧めします。スマートフォンなどでダウンロードされる場合は、ダウンロード前に「**解凍アプリ**」を**インストール**してください。
- ▶ URL は **検索ボックスではなくアドレスバー（URL 表示欄）**に入力してください。
- ▶ お使いのネットワーク環境によってはダウンロードできない場合があります。

◎ CD 00　左記の表示がある箇所の音声は、教室用 CD（Class Audio CD）に収録されています。

はじめに

　本書は、映画 *Bohemian Rhapsody*（『ボヘミアン・ラプソディ』）、*The Intern*（『マイ・インターン』）、*Moneyball*（『マネーボール』）の3作品を基にした英語総合教材である。これらの作品は、それぞれエンターテインメント、ファッション、スポーツの分野を描いており、異なる業界の作品を扱うことで、学生および教師の様々な興味・関心に対応できるようにしてある。

　本書では、それぞれの業界で見られるビジネスシーンや、様々な状況下で主人公が悩み、奮闘しながら問題解決に向けて決断を下す場面を中心に取り上げている。これらの映画を題材にすることにより、登場人物の葛藤や選択、または失敗や挑戦から、学習者も人生やキャリアについて多くのことを学ぶことができる。

　また、映画に使用される語句や口語表現の学習はもとより、映画の視聴を基にしたリスニングや背景知識を読み取るリーディングで、映画のストーリーや背景情報を知ることができる。さらに、英語の受信力を鍛えるだけでなく、内容に関する質疑応答や、セリフのシャドーイングや役柄を演じるロールプレイなどをすることによって、英語のスピーキングやインタラクションを学ぶことができる。そして、映画の字幕作成の練習を行うと同時に、映画のレビューを書くことにより、英語のライティングを含めた発信力の養成を目指す。

　映画を視聴した後には、英語のスキルだけではなく、テーマに沿って自分の意見をまとめて伝える批判的思考力の養成や、主体的な行動を促すアクティブ・ラーニングのタスクを導入している。具体例としては、個人、ペアあるいはグループで映画に関連する情報を収集したり、バンドの記者会見を開いたり、インターンの模擬面接に参加したり、自己PR動画を作成したり、スポーツファンに向けたイベントや選手のCM起用を考えたりと、学生が中心になって創造的に表現できる機会を提供する。

　本書を活用することにより、学生が映画を楽しんで視聴しながら様々な分野におけるテーマについて考え、批判的思考力を育みながら英語の4技能を伸ばす一助になることを願っている。

　最後に、本書を作成するにあたり、企画の段階から数々の助言をいただいた金星堂の福岡正人社長と企画開発室の今門貴浩氏に心より感謝を申し上げる。

2020年盛夏

著者一同

本書の構成

1作品につき5章を当てており、1章の構成は、視聴前〈Pre-viewing〉、視聴〈Movie Viewing〉、視聴後〈Post-viewing〉の3つに大きく分かれる。

視聴前 〈 Pre-viewing 〉

■ Plot Synopsis / Movie Review / Background Information: 導入の英文

各作品に関する「あらすじ」「映画の肯定的批評と否定的批評」「映画に関連する話題」のいずれかを、Unitによって100~130語程度の短い英文で紹介。

■ Vocabulary: 英日語彙選択問題

上記導入および本文から重要語彙を10語選び、英語と日本語の意味をマッチングさせる選択式問題。

■ Reading: リーディング

映画にまつわる内容を400語程度で読み、映画の登場人物や状況などの背景知識を得る。

■ Reading Comprehension: 読解問題

Unitごとに T/F問題と多肢選択式問題を交互に用い、全体の状況把握や詳細な内容把握を問う。

■ Expressions : 英語の口語表現

映画に出てくる英語の口語表現や同意語、あるいは英語表現と日本語の口語表現のマッチングなど、様々な練習問題で日常にも役立つ英語表現を学習する。

視 聴 〈 Movie Viewing 〉

■ Movie Viewing: 映画視聴

各Unitで3～4場面を取り上げ、**Dictation**（セリフの書き取り）、**Note Taking**（問題に対する情報のメモ書き）、あるいは**Listening Comprehension**（映画の聴解問題）を行う。作品によっては、**Shadowing**（シャドーイング）や**Role Play**（役になりきって演じるロールプレイ）、また**Subtitling**（日英・英日字幕作成）を導入している。

視聴後 〈 Post-viewing 〉

■ Critical Thinking & Discussion: 批判的思考およびディスカッション

批判的な思考力を養うため、映画に出てくるトピックに関して自分の意見を述べたり、ペアやグループで話し合いを行ったりする。

■ Active Learning: アクティブ・ラーニング

各Unitのテーマに関連したアクティブ・ラーニングを、個人、ペアあるいはグループで行う。授業の進捗状況や学習者のレベルに応じて、課題とするものを取捨選択して導入することができる。

■ Movie Review: 映画批評

各作品の最後のUnitには、学習者が視聴した映画についてレビューを書く活動を取り入れている。

ACTIVE ENGLISH THROUGH MOVIES

Contents

Movie ①
BOHEMIAN RHAPSODY

Movie ②
THE INTERN

Movie ③
MONEYBALL

MOVIE 1

BOHEMIAN RHAPSODY

CAST

Freddie Mercury   **Rami Malek**
Lead singer of the rock band Queen

Mary Austin   **Lucy Boynton**
Mercury's girlfriend

Brian May   **Gwilym Lee**
Roger Taylor   **Ben Hardy**
John Deacon ("Deacy")   **Joseph Mazzello**
Members of Queen

John Reid   **Aidan Gillen**
Queen's manager

Jim Beach   **Tom Hollander**
Queen's lawyer

Paul Prenter   **Allen Leech**
Mercury's personal manager

Ray Foster   **Mike Myers**
Record company executive

DIRECTED BY
Bryan Singer

◾QUEEN ◾

フレディ・マーキュリー（ボーカル）、ブライアン・メイ（ギター）、ロジャー・テイラー（ドラム）、ジョン・ディーコン（ベース）の4人で1971年にロンドンで結成されたイギリスのロックバンド。プログレッシブロック、ハードロック、ヘビーメタルからアリーナロックに至る幅広い作風とメンバーの織りなすコーラスワークで世界的な人気を博し、通算3億枚のレコードセールスを記録している。なお、本作でフレディを演じたラミ・マレックは第91回アカデミー賞®主演男優賞を受賞した。

BOHEMIAN RHAPSODY

Unit 1

Forming the Band, Queen

Queen—バンド結成

Plot Synopsis

 DL 02   CD 02

映画のあらすじを読んで、興味深いと思われる点をペアで話し合いましょう。

Anyone familiar with the music scene in the 1970s and 80s will almost certainly remember Queen. Now, a biopic of lead singer Freddie Mercury brings the joy of listening to this spectacular rock band to those of us too young to remember the real thing. Focusing on the flamboyant Mercury (Rami Malek), *Bohemian Rhapsody* tells the story of Queen's rise to fame: from playing gigs in run-down pubs to becoming one of the most successful and revered bands in the world. Despite his huge talent, Freddie's uncompromising personality and complicated personal life cause a rift with the other band members and Queen's manager, and his lifestyle begins to spiral out of control. Nevertheless, with Freddie taking center stage, Queen play one last triumphant show.

Vocabulary

DL 03   CD 03

単語の意味に合う選択肢を選んで記入しましょう（余分な選択肢が２つあります）。

1. biopic　　　　　（　）
2. flamboyant　　　（　）
3. gig　　　　　　（　）
4. run-down　　　 （　）
5. revered　　　　（　）

6. uncompromising　（　）
7. rift　　　　　　（　）
8. triumphant　　　（　）
9. comprise　　　　（　）
10. breakthrough　　（　）

a. 崇拝された	b. さびれた、荒廃した	c. 厳しい	d. 伝記映画
e. 軽蔑された	f. 不仲、亀裂	g. コンサート	h. 勝ち誇った、大成功の
i. …から構成される	j. 華やかな	k. 躍進、突破口	l. 妥協を許さない

9

Reading

映画に関する次の文を読みましょう。　　🎧 DL 04～06　💿 CD 04　～　💿 CD 06

In the late 1960s, a young college student is working part-time as a baggage handler at Heathrow airport in west London. Unknown to his colleagues, his past is almost as colorful as his future will be. Born in Zanzibar*, educated in India, the young Farrokh Bulsara had been forced to flee a violent revolution in the east

5 African island: as Zoroastrian** immigrants from India, the Bulsara family were no longer welcome in Zanzibar. Life for new arrivals in 60s Britain was not easy, and like many others at the time, Farrokh experienced some racism in his new home. Soon, however, his life was to change again, as was his name.

As a child in India, Farrokh had taken piano lessons and sung in a rock band.

10 Although he was now studying art and design, music remained his passion, and he regularly went to see London bands play in local pubs. One night, in a stroke of good fortune, Farrokh met two musicians in need of a new singer for their band, Smile. Not long afterwards, Smile had become Queen, comprising guitarist Brian May, drummer Roger Taylor, bass player John Deacon, and lead singer Freddie

15 Mercury, as Farrokh Bulsara was now known. Around the same time, as well as the new band and new name, there were other developments in Freddie's personal life. To the delight of his traditionally-minded mother, Freddie had begun a relationship with a young English woman, Mary Austin. Deeply in love, Freddie and Mary were soon engaged to be married.

20 Talented, innovative and fiercely ambitious, the members of Queen always believed they were destined for the top. Even so, success did not come without struggle. Queen needed to get themselves noticed, and to do so, Freddie decided they had to record an album. But this took money, which Queen did not have, and the only way to raise the cash was to sell their van. For a touring rock

25 band, playing different venues every night, this was a huge gamble. Thankfully for Queen, and their many fans, this gamble paid off when their album came to the attention of John Reid, a big name in the music industry who had managed many well-established stars. This was the breakthrough that Queen had been waiting for. Before long they had signed a deal with a major record company,

30 and the album hit the charts. By 1974, Queen were touring the USA, playing to sell-out crowds.

*__Zanzibar:__ アフリカ東海岸のインド洋上にあるザンジバルは 1963 年にイギリスから独立した。
**__Zoroastrian:__ 古代ペルシャを起源とするゾロアスター教の信徒。多くが迫害を逃れインドに渡った。

Reading Comprehension

本文の内容に合っているものにはT、合っていないものにはFを記入しましょう。

1. Freddie's family moved to England for financial reasons.   (   )

2. Freddie experienced some hardships after he moved to England with his family.
     (   )

3. Freddie didn't have much opportunity to study music when he was a child. (   )

4. Freddie had great passion for music, which is why he was majoring in music at college.   (   )

5. Selling their van in order to make an album was a risky decision for Queen.
     (   )

6. John Reid, who managed famous musicians, helped Queen sign a contract with a big record company.   (   )

7. After the success of their debut album, Queen toured various European cities.
     (   )

Expressions

🎧 DL 07 ◎ CD 07

ヒントと日本語表現を参考にして英語表現の空所を埋め、それぞれの表現を線を引いてマッチングさせましょう。その後で、音声をまねて感情を込めて言ってみましょう。

1. They're going **pl**__ __ __ __.	**a.** その余裕はない
2. Gotta give it a **g**__.	**b.** どんどん成功している
3. There is **r**__ __**m** for improvement.	**c.** 冒険しなくちゃ
4. We should take more **ri**__ __ __.	**d.** 何か手はあるはず
5. I'm **st**__ __**k** in the middle of nowhere.	**e.** 人里離れたところで立ち往生している
6. We can't **a**__ __ __ __**d** it.	**f.** 改善の余地はある
7. We'll find a **w**__ __.	**g.** それに賭けてみる

MOVIE VIEWING  **Dictation**

🎬 21:27-22:48

Queenのメンバーがレコード会社の大物マネージャー John Reidと日常の世話をする Paul Prenterに初めて会って話す場面を見て、空所の部分を書き取りましょう。

Reid: So, this is Queen. And you must be Freddie Mercury.

1 _____. You all have. So tell me … what makes Queen any different from all the other wannabe rock stars I meet?

Freddie: I'll tell you what it is. We're four misfits who don't belong together,

2 _____. The outcasts right at the back of the room … who are pretty sure they don't belong either.

3 _____.

Brian: We're a family.

Roger: But 4 _____.

Reid: Paul. Paul Prenter … meet Queen … our new signing. Paul will be

5 _____.

Paul: Pleasure.

Reid: If I can get you on the radio … maybe I can 6 _____.

Roger: *Top of the Pops?*

Reid: Hopefully.

Freddie: And then?

Reid: And then … it's only the biggest television program in the country. No one's ever even heard of you. Look, 7 _____.

If it goes well, if it happens … I've got 8 _____

_____.

Freddie: We'll want more.

Reid: Every band wants more.

Deacy: 9 _____.

MOVIE VIEWING  **Listening Comprehension**

🎬 22:49-24:13

QueenがBBCの番組に出演する場面を見て、次の質問に答えましょう。

1. Why does the director at the BBC tell the band to lip sync?

2. How does the director respond when Brian says, "I don't understand why we can't simply perform live"?

3. What advice does Mary give Freddie before the show?

Listening Comprehension

📽 30:01-33:27

マネージャーの**John Reid**が**Freddie**らをレコード会社の重役**Ray Foster**と弁護士**Jim Beach**に会わせてミーティングをする場面を見て、次の質問に答えましょう。

1. What does Freddie think about Jim Beach's name? What does he suggest?

2. What does Ray Foster at the record company think Queen need?

3. How does Roger respond to Ray?

4. What are two different opinions about formulas?

Freddie says	Ray Foster says

5. Things Freddie wants for the next album, *A Night at the Opera*:

- _____ record with the scale of _____,
- the pathos of _____,
- the wit of _____,
- and the unbridled joy of _____.
- It's _____.

6. How does Freddie say Queen will create the next record?

They will _____ and _____.

7. What do John Reid and Jim Beach think about Queen's new album ideas?

John Reid	Jim Beach

Critical Thinking & Discussion

22:49-24:13

Lip Sync (ロパク) 演奏について次の質問に答え、ペアやグループで意見を述べ合いましょう。

1. How would you feel if you watched a singer lip syncing?

2. What do you think is more important in a performance, perfection or authenticity?

Active Learning — Show and Tell

好きな歌手やバンドについて情報を探してまとめた後で、好きな理由を述べましょう。また、好きな歌手やバンドにまつわる個人的なエピソード (コンサートに行ったことや実際に会ったことなど) があれば、その時の記念アイテムや写真を使って経験を語りましょう。ない場合は、ネットやメディアで知った歌手やバンドにまつわるエピソードを書きましょう。

Your favorite musician/band

Musician's background information

Musician's popular songs

Reasons you like him/her/them

Anecdote about your favorite musician or band

BOHEMIAN RHAPSODY

Unit 2

Bohemian Rhapsody 「ボヘミアン・ラプソディ」誕生

Movie Review

 DL 08　　CD 08

映画の批評を読んで、その内容をペアで話し合いましょう。また、この批評家は映画にいくつ星を付けたか考えてみましょう。

Great script, great acting, and most of all, great music—*Bohemian Rhapsody* has it all! This movie will be a wonderful trip down memory lane for Queen fans, and a perfect introduction to the band for the younger generation. While Rami Malek clearly steals the show as Freddie, the supporting actors also put in great performances. Freddie's relationships with both Mary Austin and Jim Hutton are sensitively handled, and provide the emotional core of the movie. But in the end, it's all about the songs, and watching the Live Aid performance, I felt like I had travelled back in time. Without a doubt, Queen will rock you!

Vocabulary

DL 09　　CD 09

単語の意味に合う選択肢を選んで記入しましょう（余分な選択肢が２つあります）。

1. sensitively	( )	**6.** acclaim	( )
2. pan	( )	**7.** laurels	( )
3. stabilize	( )	**8.** devious	( )
4. hedonistic	( )	**9.** distrust	( )
5. mount	( )	**10.** manipulate	( )

a. 操る	**b.** 複雑な	**c.** 称賛する	**d.** 安定させる
e. よこしまな	**f.** 酷評する	**g.** 貢献する	**h.** 栄光、栄誉
i. 快楽主義の	**j.** 信頼しない	**k.** 敏感に、繊細に	**l.** 高まる、増える

15

Reading

映画に関する次の文を読みましょう。　　　🎧 DL 10 ~ 13　◉ CD 10 ~ ◉ CD 13

By 1975, Queen were at their creative peak, writing and recording *Bohemian Rhapsody*, the song which came to define them as a band. Although it was initially panned by the critics, *Bohemian Rhapsody* became hugely popular with the public, and gave the band their first number one hit. But while Queen were
5　going from strength to strength, Freddie Mercury's personal life was getting complicated.

Despite his deep love for Mary, Freddie had gradually come to the realization that he was also attracted to men, and after returning from Queen's world tour, he finally worked up the courage to admit this to Mary. While sad and disappointed,
10　in her heart Mary had already realized that Freddie was gay, and knew this was the end for them as a couple. The two of them nevertheless remained close friends, even after Mary found happiness with a new boyfriend. For Freddie though, moving on was harder. Without Mary's stabilizing influence, he fell deeper into a hedonistic rock and roll lifestyle, and began to rely more and more on his personal
15　manager, Paul Prenter, who was also gay.

Although tensions within the band were mounting, as musicians the members of Queen continued to work well together, with each contributing to the band's unique sound. By now, *Bohemian Rhapsody*, with its innovative use of opera and falsetto*, had been acclaimed as one of the most important pieces of music of the
20　1970s. Not wanting to rest on their laurels, Queen developed their music in a different direction, with the hand-clapping, foot-stamping *We Will Rock You* taking stadium rock to new levels, and delighting the band's audiences.

Behind the scenes though, all was not well. Unfortunately for Freddie, Paul proved to be a devious character, only out to promote his own interests. Clearly
25　distrusted by the other members of Queen, Paul manipulated Freddie into firing the band's long-time manager, John Reid. By doing so, he killed two birds with one stone, as removing Reid not only increased Paul's own influence, but also deepened the bad feelings between Freddie and the other members, who were angry that they had not been consulted. By 1982, it seemed that Queen were
30　reaching a crisis point.

***falsetto:** ファルセット、裏声。通常の声域より高い声で歌う唱法。

16

Reading Comprehension

本文の内容に関して正しい選択肢を選びましょう。

1. As Queen were becoming popular, what was happening to Freddie's personal life?
   a. It was becoming complicated because his fiancée was seeing somebody else while Freddie was on tour.
   b. It was becoming complex because Freddie, who was engaged to Mary, realized that he was also attracted to men.
   c. It was becoming difficult for Freddie to be away from his family for a long time.
   d. It was becoming harder for Freddie to play music without Mary's influence.

2. What is one of the unique features of the song, *Bohemian Rhapsody*?
   a. It is accompanied by hand-clapping.
   b. It invites the audience to stamp their feet.
   c. It includes operatic music with high-pitched voices.
   d. It uses a choir alongside the band.

3. What did Paul Prenter do that made the other members of Queen angry?
   a. He told the other members of Queen to fire their band manager, John Reid.
   b. He cleverly controlled Freddie in order to get rid of John Reid.
   c. He helped improve the relationship between Freddie and the other band members.
   d. He asked Freddie not to consult the other members about firing John Reid.

Expressions

🎧 DL 14　💿 CD 14

ヒントと日本語表現を参考にして英語表現の空所を埋め、それぞれの表現を線を引いてマッチングさせましょう。その後で、音声をまねて感情を込めて言ってみましょう。

1. I'm always **u__** for that.
2. It could be a **fl__p**.
3. What on **e__ __ __h** is it about?
4. This is what I always **se__ __le** for.
5. It's not even your **f__ __ __t**.
6. Anything you **fa__ __y**.
7. I didn't mean to **o__ __ __ __d** you.

a. あなたのせいではないのに
b. 失敗するかも
c. 望むところだ
d. きみが欲しいものなら何でも
e. 悪気はなかったんだ
f. それは一体何なんだ？
g. 私はいつもこうよ

MOVIE VIEWING 1 *Dictation*

🎬 42:59-44:44

Queenがレコード会社の重役Ray Fosterに会い、製作したアルバムの曲について説明する場面を見て、空所の部分を書き取りましょう。

Ray: Well … I'm not entirely sure … **¹**_____.

Freddie: No, it's better than the album we promised you. It's better than any album anyone's ever promised you, darling. It's a bloody **²**_____.

Ray: Christ.

Reid: It's **³**_____, Ray.

Roger: We prefer "masterpiece."

Ray: It's expensive, and as for … "Bohemian …"

Brian: Rhapsody.

Ray: Rhapsody. What is that?

Freddie: It's **⁴**_____.

Ray: It goes on forever. Six bloody minutes.

Freddie: I pity your wife if you think six minutes is forever. And do you know what? We're going to **⁵**_____.

Ray: Not possible. Anything over three minutes … and the radio stations won't program it, period. And **⁶**_____, anyway? Scaramouche? Galileo? And all that "Ismillah" business! "Ishmillah"?

Freddie: Bismillah.

Ray: Oh, aye. Bismillah. What's it about, anyway? Bloody Bismillah?

Freddie: True poetry is for the listener.

Brian: **⁷**_____ if everything's explained.

Ray: Seldom ruins sales. Three minutes is the standard. John.

Reid: Yeah, we need radio. Format is three minutes. I have to agree with Ray.

MOVIE VIEWING 2 *Listening Comprehension*

🎬 44:45-47:32

Queen、レコード会社重役Ray Foster、マネージャー John Reidがそれぞれシングルに選びたい曲のタイトルと理由を書きましょう。

Queen	Ray Foster
Title:	Title:
Features:	Features:
Reason:	Reason:

John Reid

Title #1: Love of My Life

Title #2:

Reason for Title #2:

MOVIE VIEWING 3 *Listening Comprehension*

Brianが新しい曲の提案をして練習している場面、実際のコンサート場面、そしてコンサート後の場面を見て、次の質問に答えましょう。

■ At the rehearsal
1:05:46-1:07:52

1. What is Brian's new idea for the next song?

2. What does Brian encourage the audience to do, besides singing along?

■ At the concert
1:07:53-1:10:00

3. What is the lyric the audience sing along with the band members?

"＿＿＿＿＿＿＿＿＿＿＿＿＿＿＿＿＿."

■ After the concert at a bar
1:10:01-1:10:44

4. What information does Paul share with John Reid at the bar?

5. Why do you think Paul suggests John Reid should mention the possible deal to Freddie?

■ After the concert in a taxi
1:12:12-1:15:07

6. Who sold 4% of all the records purchased worldwide last year?

7. What does John Reid tell Freddie?

8. How does Freddie respond to John Reid?

9. What does Freddie end up doing about John Reid?

Critical Thinking & Discussion

1:19:03-1:21:40

記者会見の場面を見て次の質問に答え、ペアやグループで意見を述べ合いましょう。

1. Do you think celebrities should answer all questions reporters ask, including about their personal lives?

2. What are some questions people may feel uncomfortable answering?

Active Learning   Press Conference

有名な海外のバンドが来日します。グループで複数の記者とバンドメンバーを決め、記者会見を開いて以下の項目を質問してください。バンドメンバーは答えたくない質問は丁寧にかわしてください。

1 Ask questions regarding the concerts or special events with fans in Japan.

-
-
-

2 Ask questions regarding things they'd like to do in Japan.

-
-
-

3 Ask questions they'll be happy to answer.

-
-
-

4 Ask questions they may not be to willing to answer.

-
-
-

5 Ask them to give messages to their fans.

BOHEMIAN RHAPSODY

Unit 3

Drifting Apart — Queen 脱退、ソロ活動へ

Movie Review

 DL 15　CD 15

映画の批評を読んで、その内容をペアで話し合いましょう。また、この批評家は映画にいくつ星を付けたか考えてみましょう。

> Rarely have I been as disappointed as after watching *Bohemian Rhapsody*. As a huge fan of Queen, I had been looking forward to this movie for a long time. Although Rami Malek is astonishingly good as Freddie, the performances of the rest of the cast are not especially memorable. Furthermore, the movie takes several liberties with the truth. In real life, Freddie's diagnosis took place in 1987, and at the time of the Live Aid concert he was still perfectly healthy. While I understand this movie is not a documentary, to change such an important part of Freddie's life story is going too far.

Vocabulary

 DL 16　CD 16

単語の意味に合う選択肢を選んで記入しましょう（余分な選択肢が2つあります）。

1. astonishingly （　）
2. diagnosis （　）
3. malign （　）
4. persistent （　）
5. bombard （　）

6. intrusive （　）
7. controversy （　）
8. outrage （　）
9. inevitable （　）
10. ensue （　）

a. 幻滅して
b. 論争、議論
c. 診断
d. しつこい、持続する
e. 避けられない、必然の
f. 善意で
g. 激しい怒り
h. 立ち入った、入り込んだ
i. 驚くほど
j. 有害な
k. 続いて起こる
l. 浴びせる、攻め立てる

Reading

映画に関する次の文を読みましょう。　　🎧 DL 17 ～ 20　💿 CD 17 ～ 💿 CD 20

　　　Encouraged by the malign influence of Paul, his personal manager, Freddie's drinking had begun to escalate, and, along with persistent rumors about his sex life, this made him an easy target for media gossip. In the early 1980s, homosexuality was not as widely accepted as it is today, and the possibility that a major star such as
5　Freddie Mercury was gay was a story that Britain's tabloid newspapers considered highly newsworthy. Rather than Queen's music, public attention now began to be centered on Freddie's personal life, and journalists at news conferences regularly ignored the other band members to bombard Freddie with offensive personal questions.

10　　　While Freddie found the media focus on his private life intrusive and unfair, neither he nor Queen were inclined to make compromises. The band courted further controversy with the video for their new single, *I Want to Break Free*, in which all four members dressed as women, complete with wigs and false breasts. For British fans, who understood that the band were imitating characters from
15　a popular drama series, the video was simply a bit of fun. In the more conservative climate of the US, however, it caused outrage, and was banned by MTV. As in the UK, most of the media attention this generated was focused on Freddie, rather than the band as a whole.

　　　Meanwhile, the musical and personal differences within the band were
20　becoming more serious, and Freddie's unreliable behavior was causing problems between him and the other three. Freddie, who was unhappy at the attention he was receiving, disillusioned with touring, and increasingly controlled by Paul, began drifting apart from the rest of Queen. Freddie's relationship with Roger, in particular, took a turn for the worse. Change, it seemed, was becoming inevitable.

25　　　In a tension-filled scene, Freddie, accompanied by Paul, announced to Brian, Roger and Deacy that he was planning to leave Queen to embark upon a solo career, and had signed a new record contract for a huge sum of money. A vicious argument ensued, with Freddie and Roger exchanging especially harsh words. When Freddie stormed out of the room it seemed that Queen's journey had come
30　to an end and Paul had got what he wanted: to have Freddie to himself.

Reading Comprehension

本文の内容に合っているものにはT、合っていないものにはFを記入しましょう。

1. As Freddie's alcohol problems escalated, his personal manager, Paul, tried to stop him from drinking. (　　)

2. As society was less tolerant of different lifestyles than today, the possibility of Freddie being gay attracted a lot of attention from the British media. (　　)

3. In the early 1980s, British tabloid newspapers began to focus on Freddie's personal life, rather than Queen's music. (　　)

4. Both British fans and American fans were upset when all members of Queen appeared on MTV dressed as women. (　　)

5. Freddie was excited about concert tours and all the attention Queen were receiving as a band. (　　)

6. The other members of Queen were happy to hear about Freddie's solo career plan since they had begun to drift apart and had lost the passion to perform as a group. (　　)

7. Paul wanted to keep Freddie under his control, and his wish came true when Freddie left the band and became a solo artist. (　　)

Expressions

🎧 DL 21　　💿 CD 21

ヒントと日本語表現を参考にして英語表現の空所を埋め、それぞれの表現を線を引いてマッチングさせましょう。その後で、音声をまねて感情を込めて言ってみましょう。

1. We can't put this **o__ __** any longer.

2. I'm the one being **b__ __ __ __d** for it.

3. I need a **b__ __ __k**.

4. I'm **s__ __ __** of it.

5. Without **t__ __ __ __ __g** us?

6. The routine is **k__ __ __ __ __g** us.

7. Are you **j__ __ __ __g**?

a. 少し休みたい

b. もううんざりだ

c. ふざけるな

d. 同じことばかりで嫌になってるだろ

e. 責められるのは俺だ

f. 無断で？

g. もう待たせられない

MOVIE VIEWING  *Dictation* 1:23:17-1:24:40

撮影したMTV（ 1:22:06-1:22:50 ）が放送禁止になったことを知り、Freddieが仕事に疲れて休みたいと話す場面を見て、空所の部分を書き取りましょう。

Freddie: MTV banned our video. The youth of America. We helped give birth to MTV.

Brian: It's America. They're **1**_____, perverts in private.

Freddie: I'm never touring in the U.S. again. And I'm the one **2**_____
_____. Not you, dear … whose idea, I believe, it was to dress up in drag. And not you. Not even you, who wrote the bloody thing. No. Crazy, cross-dressing Freddie. Freddie the freak. Freddie the fag. **3**_____. Aren't you? Album, tour, album, tour. I want to do something different.

Brian: We're a band. That's what bands do. Album, tour, album, tour.

Freddie: Well, I need a break. **4**_____.

Deacy: What are you saying, Freddie?

Freddie: **5**_____ with CBS Records.

Roger: You've done what?

Brian: Without telling us?

Deacy: **6**_____?

Freddie: Look. I'm not saying we won't record or ever tour again. **7**_____
_____. But I need to do something different. Do you know what I mean? **8**_____.

MOVIE VIEWING  *Listening Comprehension* 1:24:40-1:25:16

ソロ契約をしたと告げるFreddieとQueenのメンバーが口論になる場面を見て、次の質問に答えましょう。

1. What does Freddie say about Queen after he signed a solo contract with CBS Records?

2. How many solo albums is Freddie going to make?

3. How much did the record company pay Freddie for his solo deal?

MOVIE VIEWING 3 *Listening Comprehension* ▶ 1:25:17-1:26:58

FreddieとQueenのメンバーとの口論の続きの場面を見て、次の質問に答えましょう。

1. What are some of the arguments Queen's members have had?

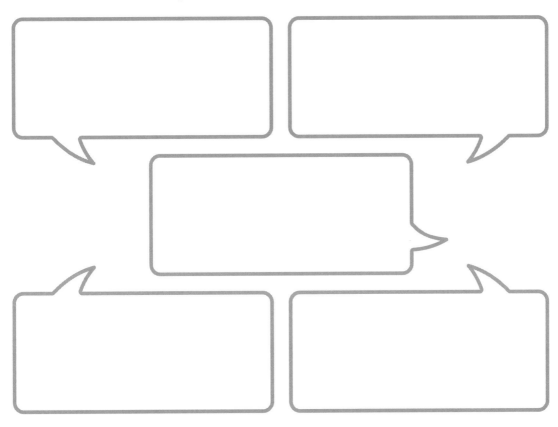

2. How does Freddie reply to Brian when he says they are a family?

3. What does Deacy say Freddie can do with the money he receives?

4. What does Freddie speculate that the other band members would be doing now if he hadn't joined Queen?

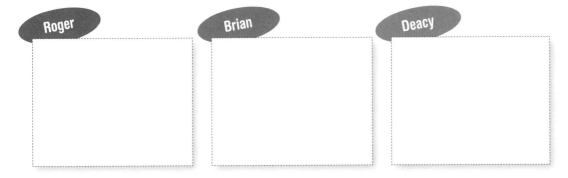

Roger   Brian   Deacy

Critical Thinking & Discussion

1:23:17-1:26:58

グループから脱退してメンバーがソロ活動することについて次の質問に答え、ペアやグループで意見を述べ合いましょう。

1. In what kind of situation do you think a band member might want to go solo?

2. What would you say to a band member who wanted to do some solo activities? Would you be against a band member signing a solo contract?

Active Learning   Planning a Concert Tour in Europe

マネージャーとして担当するバンドの2週間で2カ所を回るヨーロッパ・コンサートツアーを企画しましょう。コンサートを開く日程、国 (都市) や会場名、ホテル名、観光地などの情報を決めた後、バンドメンバーに説明しましょう。

Dates:

1st place (country, city):

Concert hall information:

Accommodation (hotel):

Days off activities (sightseeing, shopping, etc.):

Dates:

2nd place (country, city):

Concert hall information:

Accommodation (hotel):

Days off activities (sightseeing, shopping, etc.):

BOHEMIAN RHAPSODY

Unit **4**

The Truth Comes Out

マネージャーの裏切り

Background Information

DL 22　CD 22

Live Aidについて読んで、その内容をペアで話し合いましょう。

In October 1984, the BBC broadcast a graphic report about the terrible famine in Ethiopia, where drought and conflict had caused severe food shortages. The images of dying children shocked TV viewers, including the singer Bob Geldof. Geldof decided to do something to help, and with a group of other musicians, he wrote and recorded a song called *Do They Know It's Christmas?* to raise money. The song was incredibly successful, but even more money was still needed, so Geldof embarked on a bigger project—Live Aid. In July 1985, huge rock concerts were held in London and Philadelphia, with many of the world's biggest stars playing for free. The Live Aid concerts were watched by almost two billion people, and raised a vast amount of money for charity.

Vocabulary

DL 23　CD 23

単語の意味に合う選択肢を選んで記入しましょう（余分な選択肢が２つあります）。

1. famine	( )	**6.** persuade	( )
2. drought	( )	**7.** treachery	( )
3. conflict	( )	**8.** blackmail	( )
4. underway	( )	**9.** revenge	( )
5. soaked	( )	**10.** reconcile	( )

a. 裏切り	**b.** 干ばつ	**c.** 脅迫、恐喝	**d.** 仲直り・和解させる
e. ずぶ濡れの	**f.** 対立、衝突	**g.** 絶望的な	**h.** 進められている
i. 最終手段を用いる	**j.** 説得する	**k.** 飢餓	**l.** 復讐、仕返し

27

Reading

映画に関する次の文を読みましょう。　　　　🎧 DL 24 ～ 26 ◎ CD 24 ～ ◎ CD 26

　　　Newly split from Queen, and desperate to make a success of his solo career, Freddie moves to Munich with his manager, Paul, to begin work on a new album. However, writing and recording music without his bandmates is harder than he imagined. While Freddie is working all day and partying all night, back in the
5　UK preparations are underway for one of the biggest rock music events of all time. In order to raise money for the Ethiopian famine, Irish singer Bob Geldof has been recruiting musicians to play in his Live Aid concert, and has invited Queen to take part. Jim Beach, now the band's full-time manager, knows this is not a chance to be missed, and tries to call Freddie about the concert. However, Paul,
10　who wants to keep Freddie in Munich, fails to pass on Jim's messages.

　　　One stormy night when he is home alone, Freddie is astonished when his ex-girlfriend, Mary, suddenly turns up at his house. Unknown to Freddie, Mary has also been trying unsuccessfully to contact him, and is worried that he hasn't returned her calls. When Mary tells him that Jim has been trying to
15　get in touch about Live Aid, Freddie realizes that Paul has been hiding their phone calls from him. In an emotional, rain-soaked scene, Mary tries to persuade Freddie to return home. Although he lets her return to London without him, Mary's visit has opened Freddie's eyes to Paul's treachery. Devious to the last, Paul resorts to blackmail, but Freddie doesn't give in. Finally, he has seen the
20　truth behind Paul's manipulations, and wants him out of his life for good.

　　　Wanting to take revenge on Freddie for firing him, Paul goes through with his blackmail threat and gives an interview in which he tells the world about Freddie's wild lifestyle. As he watches the interview on TV, Freddie knows that he was right to get rid of Paul, and realizes it is time to go home. Meanwhile, back in
25　London, Jim Beach has given up hope of Queen playing Live Aid. However, when he finally hears from Freddie, Jim promises to do what he can to get the band back together, even though he worries that it may be too late for him to reconcile with the other band members.

Reading Comprehension

本文の内容に関して正しい選択肢を選びましょう。

1. What did Freddie do after he split from Queen?
   a. He and Paul rented a studio in the UK and recorded an album.
   b. He worked day and night with the support of Jim Beach, the band manager, to raise money for the Ethiopian famine.
   c. He left the UK with Paul and started to work on a new album.
   d. He contacted Bob Geldof and told him that he would love to participate in Live Aid.

2. What did Freddie find out when Mary visited him at his house?
   a. Jim Beach wanted Freddie to perform in Live Aid as a solo artist.
   b. Mary still loved Freddie and she wanted him to get back with her.
   c. Paul had been asking other members of Queen to perform in Live Aid.
   d. Paul intentionally hid the phone messages from Jim and Mary to Freddie.

3. What did Paul do after Freddie fired him?
   a. He revealed Freddie's wild off-stage lifestyle through a TV interview.
   b. He threatened Freddie and tried to get money from him by selling some personal pictures from parties to a publisher.
   c. He tried to take revenge on Freddie and Jim Beach and blackmailed them.
   d. He told the other members of Queen that Freddie had betrayed them.

Expressions

 DL 27　　 CD 27

ヒントと日本語表現を参考にして英語表現の空所を埋め、それぞれの表現を線を引いてマッチングさせましょう。その後で、音声をまねて感情を込めて言ってみましょう。

1. You're burning the **c__ __dl__** at both ends.
2. How **c__ __ __ __** you?
3. This has **n__ __ __ __ __ __** to do with you.
4. They're **d__ __ __ __** to meet you.
5. He'll be one **s__ __ __ __ __**.
6. I want you **o__ __** of my life.
7. You really did see **b__ __ __ __ __** the mask?

a. 彼はすぐ来る
b. よくもそんな
c. きみにどうしても会いたがってる
d. 真の姿を見たんですね
e. 働きすぎよ
f. 二度と顔を見せるな
g. あなたには関係ない

MOVIE VIEWING ① *Subtitling*

▶ 1:26:59-1:27:29

次の日本語を英語にしましょう。その後で、実際にどのような表現が使われているか場面を見てみましょう。

ポール：	もしもし？	_____
メアリー：	ポール　フレディに話できる？	_____
ポール：	ああ メアリー	_____
	いや、いま彼は話せない	_____
	昼も夜もずっと働いている	_____
メアリー：	電話したことを必ず伝えて	_____
ポール：	ご心配なく	_____
	彼なら大丈夫だから	_____
	電話があったと必ず伝える	_____
	じゃあ	_____

MOVIE VIEWING ② *Dictation*

▶ 1:27:55-1:28:21

Queenの新しいマネージャー Jim Beachが Freddieの個人マネージャー Paul Prenterに電話する場面を見て、空所の部分を書き取りましょう。

Beach: Where is he? Is he there? I wanna speak to him.

Paul: He is working **1**_____. I'm blue in the face trying to get him to take a break.

Beach: Paul, listen to me. It's one performance for a good cause. It's a televised concert for the famine in Ethiopia. They're gonna have **2**_____ _____ in Philadelphia and London. There's gonna be **3**_____ watching. Queen should be part of it.

Paul: He's just been really focused. But **4**_____.

Beach: Sure you will.

 **Listening Comprehension**   1:28:45-1:33:42

MaryがドイツにいるFreddieに会いに行き、初めてPaulの企みをFreddieが知る場面を見て、次の質問に答えましょう。

1. What does Mary tell Freddie that Jim Beach is trying to do?

2. How does Mary describe Live Aid to Freddie?

3. Why does Freddie think Paul has not told him about Live Aid?

4. What does Freddie want Mary to do?

5. How does Mary respond to Freddie?

6. What does Mary say about Paul?

7. What does Mary tell Freddie to do?

 **Listening Comprehension**   1:33:43-1:36:43

FreddieとPaulが言い合う場面を見て、次の質問に答えましょう。

1. How does Paul respond to Freddie's question about not telling him about Live Aid?

2. What does Freddie do after he finds out about Paul's manipulation?

3. What does Paul do after he is no longer working for Freddie?

Critical Thinking & Discussion 🎬 1:33:43-1:36:43

Paulが FreddieにLive Aidのことを隠していたことについて次の質問に答え、ペアやグループで意見を述べ合いましょう。

1. Why do you think Paul hides the information about Live Aid from Freddie?

2. What would you do if you found out that your manager was doing something behind your back and trying to exploit you?

Active Learning   Promotional Campaign

ペアを組み、アーティスト役とマネージャー役を決めましょう。マネージャーはアーティストの参加するチャリティーイベントを決め、告知するポスターを作成しましょう。アーティストは情報番組でその内容を宣伝しましょう。ポスターにはできる範囲で画像も入れてみましょう。

Creation of a poster about the charity event	Announcement of the charity event
as a manager	**as an artist**

Name of the charity event:

Purpose of the charity event:

Date:

Venue:

Who else would be expected to attend:

BOHEMIAN RHAPSODY

Unit 5

Performing in Live Aid   Live Aid での圧巻のパフォーマンス

Background Information

🎧 DL 28   ◎ CD 28

Freddieを演じたRami Malekについて読んで、その内容をペアで話し合いましょう。

Although acting seems a glamorous profession, in reality it involves enormous dedication. Rami Malek, who plays Freddie Mercury in *Bohemian Rhapsody*, has been widely praised, and Queen guitarist Brian May has even said that he sometimes forgot that Rami was not really Freddie! However, to play such an iconic figure so convincingly requires not only talent, but also a lot of hard work. Rami spent hundreds of hours watching videos of Queen performing, and took singing, dancing and piano lessons. As if this was not challenging enough, he also had to learn to speak and sing wearing a special set of false teeth in order to look more like Freddie. His effort was worth it though, as Rami rightly ended up collecting an Oscar for his stunning performance.

Vocabulary

🎧 DL 29   ◎ CD 29

単語の意味に合う選択肢を選んで記入しましょう（余分な選択肢が２つあります）。

1. glamorous	( )	**6.** convince	( )
2. iconic	( )	**7.** apprehensive	( )
3. figure	( )	**8.** rusty	( )
4. stunning	( )	**9.** confirm	( )
5. contrite	( )	**10.** incurable	( )

a. 納得させる	**b.** 確認する	**c.** 疑いなく	**d.** さびた、下手になった
e. 人物、姿	**f.** 華やかな	**g.** 象徴的な	**h.** 見事な、素晴らしい
i. 不治の、治らない	**j.** 偽の、作り上げた	**k.** 悔いている	**l.** 不安な、心配している

33

Reading

映画に関する次の文を読みましょう。　　　DL 30 ～ 33　CD 30 ～ CD 33

A year on from the meeting in which Freddie quit Queen, the four band members are once again together in the same room. In Jim Beach's office, a contrite Freddie admits to the others that he was wrong to leave and that his solo career has been a failure. After some tense moments, Queen forgive Freddie and allow him to rejoin the band. But problems remain. Although Jim and Freddie eventually convince the others to play Live Aid, they haven't performed together for years and are apprehensive about taking on such a huge concert with little time to rehearse.

When rehearsals begin, it seems that the band's fears were well-founded. Freddie's voice is rusty, and Queen have lost the old magic. Soon though, they discover that worries about performing poorly are far from their biggest concern. Freddie had been ill for a while, and after returning to London, a visit to the doctor confirmed his worst fear. During a particularly poor rehearsal, Freddie announces to the others that he has been diagnosed with AIDS, which at that time was incurable. Despite their shock, the band agree that "the show must go on," and that Freddie's illness will not stop them playing the show of their lives at Live Aid.

On the day of the concert, the whole world is watching. But before he goes on stage, there is something Freddie needs to do. Several years ago, he had met a man he liked at a party, and had been searching for him ever since. Having finally found Jim Hutton's address, Freddie knocks on his door and invites him to Wembley Stadium to watch the Live Aid performance. A few hours later, watched by Jim and Mary, his family at home, and millions of people across the world, Freddie took to the stage. And on a day in which the world's biggest stars all performed, Queen were to shine brightest of all.

As a musician, Live Aid was undoubtedly the peak of Freddie Mercury's career. Sadly though, six years later in 1991, Freddie died at just 45 years old. However, these last years, reconciled with his bandmates and in a stable relationship with Jim, were some of the happiest of his life. And as the success of the *Bohemian Rhapsody* movie proved, Freddie Mercury may be gone, but he will never be forgotten.

Reading Comprehension

本文の内容に合っているものには**T**、合っていないものには**F**を記入しましょう。

1. Freddie regretted that he had left Queen and asked the other band members if he could rejoin the band. ( )

2. Although his solo career has been successful, Freddie felt that he wanted to play in Live Aid as a member of Queen. ( )

3. It was not difficult for Jim Beach and Freddie to convince the other band members to play in Live Aid, since they were enthusiastic about this charity event. ( )

4. Once rehearsals began, Queen were easily able to rediscover the old magic they used to have. ( )

5. Although Freddie found out that he had a serious health condition, he decided not to tell the band members till Live Aid was over. ( )

6. On the day of Live Aid, Freddie found Jim Hutton, a man he had met at a party and liked, and invited him to the concert. ( )

7. Freddie passed away several years after Live Aid but as the popularity of the movie proves, his legacy will be remembered. ( )

Expressions

🎧 DL 34 💿 CD 34

ヒントと日本語表現を参考にして英語表現の空所を埋め、それぞれの表現を線を引いてマッチングさせましょう。その後で、音声をまねて感情を込めて言ってみましょう。

1. I've been **con__ __ __ __ed**.

2. Name your **t__ __ms**.

3. I just felt **l__ __ __ it**.

4. On what **pre__ __xt**?

5. For right now it's **b__ __ __ __ __n us**.

6. Don't **f__ __s about it**.

7. I could **d__ with a friend**.

a. 口実は？

b. 条件を言ってほしい

c. そのことで怒らないこと

d. 友だちが必要なんだ

e. ただなんとなく

f. うぬぼれていた

g. 今のところ俺たちだけの秘密だ

MOVIE VIEWING **1** *Listening Comprehension*

1:38:12-1:41:56

Queenのメンバーが再会してFreddieが許しを請い、グループとして活動を再開するための条件をメンバーが提示する場面を見て、次の質問に答えましょう。

1. What did the other members of Queen decide on as the terms for getting back together and performing again?

2. Aside from making music together, what is one problem the other members of Queen mention to Freddie?

3. What did Freddie do to solve that problem?

MOVIE VIEWING **2** *Listening Comprehension*

1:41:57-1:43:24

Jim BeachがLive Aidについて説明する場面を見て、次の質問に答えましょう。

1. Write down the following information you hear about Live Aid.

The number of people expected at Wembley Stadium: _____

The number of people expected at JFK Stadium in Philadelphia: _____

The number of countries the TV show is being broadcast in: _____

The number of satellites used: _____

The size of the global TV audience: _____

The length of the set for each group: _____

2. What does Freddie say about not participating in Live Aid?

MOVIE VIEWING 3 *Listening Comprehension*

🎬 1:46:05-1:47:57

Live Aidに向けたリハーサルとその後の場面を見て、次の質問に答えましょう。

1. Why didn't the rehearsal go well?

2. How much time do Queen have before Live Aid?

3. What does Freddie tell the other members of Queen after the rehearsal?

4. What expression does Freddie use when he wants to keep the news secret?

   " _____ "

5. What does Freddie not want the others to do about his condition?

   He does not want them to _____ about it or _____ about it.

   He does not want any _____ from them.

6. What does Freddie want to do with the time he has left?

7. What does Freddie not want to be in the time he has left?

   their _____, their _____,

   or their _____.

MOVIE VIEWING 4 *Subtitling*

🎬 1:47:58-1:48:20

次のセリフの日本語字幕を1行13字以内で作成しましょう。その後で、字幕では実際にどのような表現が使われているか場面を見てみましょう。また、Freddieになりきって演じてみましょう。

English Script	Japanese Subtitle
Freddie: I decide who I am.	_____
I'm going to be	_____
what I was born to be.	_____
A performer …	_____
who gives the people	_____
what they want.	_____
Touch of the heavens.	_____

Critical Thinking & Discussion

1:38:12-1:41:56

グループ解散後の再活動の可能性やチャリティー活動などについて次の質問に答え、ペアやグループで意見を述べ合いましょう。

1. Do you think a band that has split up could ever get back together? If so, under what circumstances? Do you know any bands which got back together after once splitting up?

2. If you were a musician, would you like to participate in any charity events? If so, which ones?

Active Learning   Movie Review

映画*Bohemian Rhapsody*について、各項目をチェック☑しながら評価して星の数を決めた後で、自分なりに批評（映画のよい点や不満な点）を英語で書きましょう。

Rating Criteria	1 ××	2 ×	3 △	4 ○	5 ◎
Plot / Story Development					
Main Cast: Acting / Performance					
Supporting Cast: Acting / Performance					
Scenes / Situations / Setting					
Cinematography / Camerawork					
Script / Language					
Music / Sound Effects					

Movie Review   Stars ☆ ☆ ☆ ☆ ☆

MOVIE 2

THE INTERN

CAST

Ben Whittaker　**Robert De Niro**

Seventy-year-old senior intern at an online fashion company

Jules Ostin　**Anne Hathaway**

Founder and CEO of "About The Fit," online fashion startup in Brooklyn

Cameron　**Andrew Rannells**

Jules' assistant

Becky　**Christina Scherer**

Jules' secretary

Matt　**Anders Holm**

Jules' husband

DIRECTED BY
Nancy Myers

■ROBERT DE NIRO■

1943年、アメリカ・ニューヨーク生まれ。「デ・ニーロ・アプローチ」と呼ばれる徹底した役作りで知られ、実在のボクサー役を演じた『レイジング・ブル』(80) でアカデミー賞®主演男優賞、『ゴッドファーザー PART II』(74) で同助演男優賞を受賞。その他の代表作に『タクシードライバー』(76)、『ディア・ハンター』(78)、『キング・オブ・コメディ』(83)、『ワンス・アポン・ア・タイム・イン・アメリカ』(84)、『アンタッチャブル』(87)、『グッドフェローズ』(90) などがある。近年でも『ジョーカー』(19)、『アイリッシュマン』(19) で存在感を示している。

■ANNE HATHAWAY■

1982年、アメリカ・ニューヨーク生まれ。2001年に『プリティ・プリンセス』でデビュー。その後、『ブロークバック・マウンテン』(05)、『プラダを着た悪魔』(06) などを経て、『レイチェルの結婚』(08) でアカデミー賞®主演女優賞にノミネート、『レ・ミゼラブル』(12) で同助演女優賞を受賞。その他の出演作に『アリス・イン・ワンダーランド』シリーズ、『ダークナイト・ライジング』(12)、『インターステラー』(14) などがある。

©Collection Christophel via AFP

Plot Synopsis

🎧 DL 35　◎ CD 35

映画のあらすじを読んで、興味深いと思われる点をペアで話し合いましょう。

In today's aging society, *The Intern* is a tale for our times. Ben Whitaker (Robert De Niro) is a 70-year-old widower, bored with life after retirement and longing to return to a more active role. Ben, who worked in the world of business for many years, is accepted as a senior intern at a fashion company, against the wishes of its young CEO, Jules Ostin (Anne Hathaway). At first, Jules views Ben as a nuisance—an outdated old man who has no place in her modern, forward-looking company. Yet as she gets to know him, Jules realizes the value of Ben's experience and wisdom, and comes to depend on him as both an employee and a friend.

Vocabulary

🎧 DL 36　◎ CD 36

単語の意味に合う選択肢を選んで記入しましょう（余分な選択肢が２つあります）。

1. widower	( )	6. accumulate	( )
2. retirement	( )	7. idyllic	( )
3. nuisance	( )	8. punctuate	( )
4. outdated	( )	9. bolster	( )
5. employee	( )	10. flyer	( )

a. 退職	b. 貯める、累積する	c. 従業員	d. のどかな
e. 強化する	f. 厄介なもの・人	g. チラシ	h. 旧式の、時代遅れの
i. 雇い主	j. 差し挟む	k. 夫を亡くした女性	l. 妻を亡くした男性

Reading

映画に関する次の文を読みましょう。　🎧 DL 37 ~ 40　💿 CD 37 ~ 💿 CD 40

On paper, it appears that 70-year old Ben Whitaker has a rich and fulfilling life. After retiring from work, he has spent his time playing golf, doing tai-chi, learning Mandarin and traveling the world with the air miles he has accumulated. For many of us, this might sound like an idyllic existence, but for Ben it is not enough. Since his
5　wife died three-and-a-half years ago, he has felt there is something missing in his life. Having tried his best to become accustomed to the rhythms of life as a widowed pensioner, with its constant round of funerals punctuated only by the occasional visit to his son's family in San Diego, Ben realizes that something needs to change.

Like many companies, the successful new internet fashion retailer About
10　The Fit (ATF) regularly offers unpaid internships to young people, usually college students, to enable them to gain valuable work experience and bolster their resumés. Recently, however, the company has introduced an internship with a difference. Cameron, the assistant to the CEO of ATF, has seen an opportunity to promote the company's image by hiring senior citizen interns
15　as part of a community outreach program*. But while Cameron is enthusiastic about the plan, Jules Ostin, the young CEO of the company, is more reluctant.

On his way home from grocery shopping one morning, Ben spots a flyer advertising the senior intern program at ATF and realizes this might be just the opportunity he needs to reboot his life. Although Ben has no experience of
20　e-commerce, he meets all the other requirements of the advertisement. Before retiring, Ben had a long and successful career in business, working for a company that made telephone directories. Over his 40 years in the job, he was responsible for advertising, sales and printing, and eventually rose to be Vice President of the company.

25　Reading the flyer with his friend Patty, Ben realizes that the business world has changed since his retirement. In order to apply for the internship, Ben needs to make a video of himself to upload to YouTube, instead of sending a traditional cover letter. However, Ben is not put off by the challenges of new technology and modern working styles, and his positive response to the complicated application
30　process demonstrates the attitude that ATF requires of its interns.

*community outreach program:** 地域での雇用促進プログラム、地域への貢献活動

Reading Comprehension

本文の内容に合っているものにはT、合っていないものにはFを記入しましょう。

1. After retirement, Ben played golf, took up Chinese and learned a Chinese martial art. ( )

2. Ben enjoys living with his son and his family in San Diego, California. ( )

3. After Ben retired, he enjoyed traveling around the world, paying for the airfares with his pension. ( )

4. ATF is a newly established company that sells clothes online. ( )

5. Both Jules, CEO of ATF, and her assistant, Cameron, are excited about implementing an internship program for senior citizens. ( )

6. Ben has a lot of work experience in sales, advertising and printing, but not in online business. ( )

7. In order to apply for an internship at ATF, Ben needs to submit a video with his self-introduction. ( )

Expressions

日本語の意味に合うように空所に適切な語を入れて文を完成させましょう。

1. 退職後、私はどこに行く必要もなく、ずる休みをしているように感じました。
   After _____, I didn't have to go _____, and I felt like I was _____ hooky.

2. 雨が降っていても晴れていても、私は毎日朝散歩をすることを日課にしています。
   Come _____ or _____, I make a _____ of taking a walk every morning.

3. 誤解しないでください。私は自分のすることを毎日楽しんでいます。
   Don't _____ me _____. I enjoy _____ I do every day.

4. 店のそばを通りかかったとき、御社のチラシが目の端に留まりました。
   When I was _____ by the store, I caught your _____ out of the _____ of my eye.

5. 今回は食事に行けませんが、この次また誘ってくださいますか。
   I can't go to dinner this time, so can I _____ a _____ _____?

MOVIE VIEWING ① *Note Taking*

▶️ 4:36-5:43

Benがインターンに応募するために自己PRのカバーレター動画を作成する場面を見て、以下のポイントに注意してメモを取りましょう。その後で、ペアやグループでBenの紹介をしてみましょう。

Reasons Ben is applying for a senior internship

Ben's weakness

Ben's strength

Ben's work experience

Ben's comments on his hometown

The quote Ben read about musicians and his comments about himself

MOVIE VIEWING ② *Note Taking*

🎬 6:23-7:11

顧客からの電話クレームに対処する場面を見て、クレームの内容とCEOのJulesの対応について以下のポイントに注意してメモを取りましょう。

- **The original order the customer, Rachel, made for her six bridesmaids:**

  Six _____ chiffon Antoinette dresses in _____

- **The wedding** will be in _____ days.

- **The wrong items Rachel received:**

  Six chiffon Antoinette dresses in charcoal _____

- **Jules' actions to solve the problem: She is going to …**

  ❶ call _____ and have this fixed _____.

  ❷ personally _____ before they are _____.

  ❸ promise the customer that they will be at her _____ by

  _____.

  ❹ give the customer her phone number: _____-_____-_____

  ❺ _____.

MOVIE VIEWING ③ *Listening Comprehension*

🎬 7:12-7:56

秘書のBeckyがJulesにスケジュールを伝える場面を見て、次の質問に答えましょう。

1. When will Cameron be back in the office today?

2. What do the staff working on tomorrow's homepage need Jules to do?

3. Where does Jules need to be at 11:00?

4. What idea does Jules want Becky to email her?

5. How does Jules respond to Becky's question about calling her mother back?

6. What aspect of staff behavior in the office does Jules complain about?

45

Critical Thinking & Discussion

2:55-4:02

Benがシニアインターンの求人広告について友人のPattyと話す場面を見て次の質問に答え、企業の採用方法に関してペアやグループで意見を述べ合いましょう。

1. Have you heard of a cover letter video for a job application before? Would you like to apply for an internship that requires you to submit a cover letter video?

2. What do you think employers are looking for when they view applicants' cover letter videos, compared with their written résumés?

Active Learning — Making a Cover Letter Video

自己PRのカバーレター動画を作成するために、次の質問に答えましょう。そこから出てきたキーワードを用いて自己分析してみましょう。

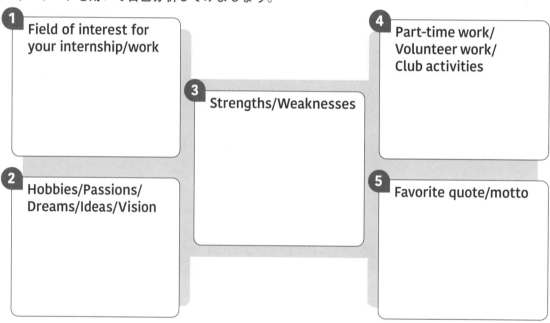

1 Field of interest for your internship/work

2 Hobbies/Passions/ Dreams/Ideas/Vision

3 Strengths/Weaknesses

4 Part-time work/ Volunteer work/ Club activities

5 Favorite quote/motto

キーワードに基づいて自己PR文を書き（150〜200語）、原稿を読む練習をしてから1分程度の動画を作成しましょう。

©Collection Christophel via AFP

THE INTERN

Unit 7

The Working Environment at ATF ATF 社の職場環境

Movie Review 🎧 DL 41 💿 CD 41

映画の批評を読んで、その内容をペアで話し合いましょう。また、この批評家は映画にいくつ星を付けたか考えてみましょう。

> *The Intern* is touching and funny in equal measure. Robert De Niro, one of the world's leading actors for over forty years, is outstanding as Ben, proving the central point of the film that increasing age does not equal decreasing ability. Anne Hathaway also gives a fine performance, portraying Jules with a combination of confidence and vulnerability that makes her a sympathetic character, rather than an irritating one. The chemistry between the two leads is perfect, and the audience is soon drawn into their story. *The Intern* is a feel-good movie to appeal to all generations, and you are guaranteed to leave the theater happier than when you arrived.

Vocabulary 🎧 DL 42 💿 CD 42

単語の意味に合う選択肢を選んで記入しましょう（余分な選択肢が2つあります）。

1. outstanding （　）
2. vulnerability （　）
3. sympathetic （　）
4. irritating （　）
5. chemistry （　）

6. guarantee （　）
7. quirk （　）
8. idiosyncratic （　）
9. emulate （　）
10. delegate （　）

a. 保証する	b. 張り合う	c. 取引	d. 委任する
e. 弱さ、もろさ	f. 相性	g. 特有の、独特の	h. 傑出した、すば抜けた
i. 同情的な	j. 貢献する	k. イライラさせる	l. おかしな癖、特異な行動

Reading

映画に関する次の文を読みましょう。　　　🎧 DL 43 ~ 45　◉CD 43 ~ ◉CD 45

　　Hiring a 70-year old as an intern is, to say the least, a little unusual. But as Ben discovers during the first day of his internship, the "brave new world" of e-commerce is very different to the traditional workplace that he is used to. Many recent success stories seem to have their famous quirks: it is well-known that
5　Steve Jobs of Apple wore the same type of black turtleneck every day, that Google employees have dedicated sleeping zones in their workplaces, and that Amazon's Jeff Bezos bans his employees from using PowerPoint in meetings. And while About The Fit (ATF) is a newer and smaller company, it has working methods that are no less idiosyncratic, and is well on the way to emulating the success of
10　these global giants.

　　Started just a year and a half ago in Jules Ostin's kitchen, ATF has expanded rapidly and now boasts over 200 employees in a trendy open plan office space in the Brooklyn district of New York. Jules is far from a typical CEO, and instead of sitting in a boardroom negotiating with other high-powered executives, spends
15　time manning the phone lines along with her staff. Her hands-on approach even extends to personally dealing with customer complaints, and rather than delegating tasks from a luxurious private office, Jules prefers to be actively involved in every detail of running the company. Nevertheless, this does not mean that Jules is always an easy-going and approachable boss. Her over-worked secretary, Becky,
20　seems terrified of her, and can regularly be found jogging across the office to keep up with Jules, who rides a bicycle between the desks to save a few precious minutes of her time.

　　Jules' personal behavior seems to set the tone for the company as a whole, where things are generally done slightly differently. When the company, or an individual
25　employee, achieves something special, a bell is rung, and an announcement of the good news is made to all the staff. This is just one of many unconventional ways that ATF tries to create a fun and relaxing working environment. During the working day, while other employees are at their computers, one group of staff hold a birthday party in the middle of the office, complete with cake, presents and balloons. And
30　certainly anybody who had spent most of their career at a more traditional company would be pleasantly surprised at the offer of a free massage while sitting at their desk!

Reading Comprehension

本文の内容に関して正しい選択肢を選びましょう。

1. Based on the information in the reading, which of the following sentences is true?
   a. E-commerce and traditional workplaces have a lot in common.
   b. Leaders in both new and traditional workplaces wear suits and ties.
   c. Employees in neither new nor traditional workplaces are allowed to nap at work.
   d. The workplaces at ATF and a traditional company differ tremendously.

2. How does Jules run her company, ATF?
   a. She delegates tasks to her staff from a luxurious private office.
   b. She and her staff ride bicycles and jog together to discuss issues.
   c. She is involved with daily business operations, including customer service.
   d. She spends most of her time in a boardroom negotiating with other executives.

3. What do they do at ATF when the company or an employee achieves something special?
   a. They throw parties and celebrate the good news after work.
   b. They ring a bell and announce the good news.
   c. They announce the good news and give presents.
   d. They ask employees to give presentations about their achievement.

Expressions

日本語の意味に合うように（　　）内の語句を並べ替えて文を完成させましょう。

1. 私は昨年、宣伝部の責任者でした。
   (advertising / was / overseeing / department / in charge of / the / last year)
   I _____.

2. あなたはこの仕事をするのに十二分の資格があるようです。
   (to / qualified / job / this / more than / seem / for / be)
   You _____.

3. あなたは数カ月後に営業部に配属されます。
   (the / a few months / assigned / in / to / department / will / sales / be)
   You _____.

MOVIE VIEWING ① *Note Taking*

📹 9:30-11:09

Benが面接官から質問を受ける場面を見て、以下のポイントに注意してメモを取りましょう。

1. The university Ben graduated from

The year Ben graduated from his university

2. The name of the company Ben worked for after graduation

The product the company made

3. Ben was in charge of

Ben was the VP of

4. What is the one big question the male interviewer usually asks of their intern candidates?

5. What does the male interviewer think of Ben?

MOVIE VIEWING ② *Note Taking*

📹 13:01-14:39

ATF社の始まりや特徴について、以下のポイントに注意してメモを取りましょう。

1. When did Jules start the company? _____

2. Where was Jules' idea hatched? _____

3. When did ATF start online business? _____

4. How many employees did ATF initially have? _____

5. How many employees, including interns, does ATF have now? _____

6. How many "likes" on Instagram did ATF receive? _____

7. How do interns get information regarding their jobs? _____

MOVIE VIEWING ③ *Listening Comprehension* 🎬 14:40-19:33

インターンの配属先が判明し、秘書のBeckyからアドバイスをもらったBenがCEOのJules
と初めて会う場面を見て、次の質問に答えましょう。

1. Which sections are the new interns going to be working in?

Ben	Female intern	Male intern
_____	_____	_____

2. What time does Ben have an appointment with Jules Ostin?

_____

3. How old is Ben? How about Becky?

Ben: _____   Becky: _____

4. What is some of the advice Becky gives to Ben?

-
-
-

5. According to Jules, why is Ben being assigned to her?

6. Which section does Jules think Ben is suitable for? Why?

7. How does Jules describe herself?

8. How does Ben describe himself?

9. What would Ben like to do?

Critical Thinking & Discussion

16:42-17:32

面接に関するアドバイスの場面を見て次の質問に答え、ペアやグループで意見を述べ合いましょう。

1. Have you received any advice before you went for an important interview? Who did you receive advice from? What kind of advice did you receive?

2. What kind of advice would you give to a friend who is going to have a job interview for a part-time job, an internship, or a full-time job?

Active Learning   A Mock Interview

グループで面接官数名と求職者を決め、模擬面接を行いましょう。職種や求めている人材もグループで決め、面接後に求職者に関してよかった点と改善する必要のある点を話し合いましょう。

Interview sample questions

Q1. Why are you applying for this job at our company?

Q2. What do you study at school? What's your major?

Q3. Have you acquired any qualifications?

Q4. Could you tell us about yourself? Why do you think you fit this company?

Q5. What are some of the unique experiences you've had in university? What did you learn from those experiences? What makes you different from others?

以下の評価基準を使って求職者を評価しましょう。

Evaluation criteria (1-5 points each)					
1	2	3	4	5	
Knowledge/ Skills (5)	Personality/ Attitude (5)	Communi- cation (5)	Adaptablity/ Flexibility (5)	Fit for Company (5)	Total (25)
Scores					
Comments					

The Problems ATF Faces　成長する ATF 社の抱える問題

©Collection Christophel via AFP

Movie Review

 DL 46　 CD 46

映画の批評を読んで、その内容をペアで話し合いましょう。また、この批評家は映画にいくつ星を付けたか考えてみましょう。

Despite calling on the talents of two exceptional actors, *The Intern* is a dull and predictable movie. The basic scenario of a pensioner working as an intern feels rather implausible, as do specific scenes such as Jules cycling through the open plan office. While both main characters are likeable, they seem one-dimensional, and it is hard to care what happens to either of them. The dialogue is slow and sentimental, and the plot offers no surprises: it is obvious from very early in the film that Jules will change her opinion of Ben and they will bond in some way. If you need to pass the time on a long plane journey, then *The Intern* would do the job. But don't shell out good money to go to see it.

Vocabulary

DL 47　 CD 47

単語の意味に合う選択肢を選んで記入しましょう（余分な選択肢が２つあります）。

1. exceptional	(　　)	6. initiative	(　　)
2. implausible	(　　)	7. bug	(　　)
3. shell out	(　　)	8. reassuring	(　　)
4. anonymous	(　　)	9. insight	(　　)
5. menial	(　　)	10. anticipate	(　　)

a. 率先	b. つまらない	c. 安心できる	d. 並外れた
e. 匿名の	f. 支払う	g. 困らせる、悩ませる	h. 割り当てる
i. 信じがたい	j. 予想する	k. 同行する	l. 洞察

53

Reading

映画に関する次の文を読みましょう。　　　🎧 DL 48 ~ 51　◎CD 48 ~ ◎CD 51

　　When he begins work at About The Fit (ATF), Ben has little idea of what to expect. Despite his long years of experience, the role of "senior intern" is clearly going to be very different from any other he has fulfilled. For example, the very first person Ben meets at the company uses the term "talent acquisition" instead
5　of personnel department, which is not a phrase that Ben has ever heard before.

　　Soon after this, Ben discovers that, unlike the anonymous backroom roles assigned to the other interns, he will be spending his six weeks at the company as a personal intern to company founder Jules Ostin. When Ben meets Jules, he learns that not only is she unsure what his role will be, but also that she doesn't
10　really want a personal intern at all. Their first meeting takes only two minutes, and Jules suggests there will be little that Ben can help her out with. In his first few days at the company, while everyone around him seems rushed off their feet, Ben is left twiddling his thumbs. Soon though, Ben finds ways to make himself useful to the other employees, and before he knows it they are relying on him for
15　help and advice.

　　Jules herself finally finds some work for Ben, but only gives him menial and unsatisfying tasks such as doing her dry cleaning. However, when Ben takes the initiative to sort out a problem which has been bugging Jules for weeks, she realizes that perhaps she could be making more use of his talents and experience. Before
20　long, Ben has taken over as Jules' driver, and she gradually comes to appreciate his reassuring presence and begins to give him more meaningful and challenging tasks.

　　With his business experience, Ben is able to provide insights and solve problems that the rest of the team are struggling with. He volunteers to accompany Jules
25　on business trips, and she starts to rely more and more on his advice. But Ben doesn't just help Jules with business—he even ends up taking care of her daughter. And when Jules' careless mistake leads to a personal crisis, Ben leads the other interns on a daring mission to save the day. Life as an intern turns out to be more varied and exciting than Ben had anticipated!

Reading Comprehension

本文の内容に合っているものにはT、合っていないものにはFを記入しましょう。

1. Since Ben has a lot of work experience, he knows what to expect when he starts to work as a senior intern. ( )

2. Ben is not familiar with the term "talent acquisition," which refers to the personnel department. ( )

3. Jules is hesitant to hire a personal intern and she is not sure what Ben can actually do for her. ( )

4. Every intern is assigned a job and gets busy from day one of their work. ( )

5. Although Ben is initially given an insignificant task that does not require his skills or talents, he starts to help out around the office voluntarily. ( )

6. As Jules notices Ben's capabilities, she asks him to get involved in more important tasks. ( )

7. Jules begins to rely more on Ben and asks him to help her with personal matters, but he refuses to work for her outside of the office. ( )

Expressions

日本語の意味に合うように空所に適切な語を入れて文を完成させましょう。

1. 誰もが新しい CEO 候補が会社経営の経験が乏しい点を心配しています。

   Everybody is _____ that the new CEO is _____ at _____ a company.

2. 私にとって新しい技術についていくのが大変です。

   It's hard for me to _____ _____ _____ new technology.

3. 我が社の製品の見込み客のリストを作成しました。

   I made a list of _____ _____ for our _____.

4. この会議で耳にすることはすべて極秘です。

   _____ you hear in this meeting is _____ _____.

5. 今度の金曜日にパーティーをします。ぜひ来てください。

   We're having a party this _____ Friday. Be _____ or be _____.

MOVIE VIEWING 1 *Note Taking*

23:42-25:31

新たなCEOを外部から招く提案について質問するJulesに対して、アシスタントのCameronがATF社の抱える問題を指摘する場面を見て、以下のポイントに注意してメモを取りましょう。

---

1. What are some of the issues Jules worries that the investors might have with her?

Jules' experience	Jules' school	Jules' methods

2. Although the company hit its 5-year goal in 9 months, what are some of the problems Jules and ATF are facing, according to Cameron?

ATF: _____.

Jules: _____.

Tech staff: _____.

Customer Service: _____.

Other problems:

-
-
-

3. What does Cameron say will happen to the problems if the company gets bigger?

4. What do investors think a seasoned CEO could do?

MOVIE VIEWING 2  *Listening Comprehension* 32:41-33:12

JulesとCameronがCEO候補のAtwoodについて話す場面を見て、次の質問に答えましょう。

1. Which companies did Atwood manage before?

_____ _____

2. What does Jules think about Atwood?

3. What has Atwood been doing about ATF? How does Atwood like ATF?

4. What advice does Cameron give to Jules about Atwood?

5. According to Cameron, how do venture capitalists (VCs) like Atwood?

6. What does Jules say about Mark Zuckerberg, the CEO of Facebook?

MOVIE VIEWING 3  *Listening Comprehension* 34:05-35:07

JulesがCEOの候補者に会った後に感想を述べる場面を見て、次の質問に答えましょう。

1. What did Jules think of Atwood?

2. What would Jules' two major concerns about Atwood be if he ran ATF?

-
-

3. What else didn't Jules like about Atwood?

Critical Thinking & Discussion

▶ 23:42-25:31

新たなCEOを雇う可能性について探るシーンをもう一度見て次の質問に答え、自分の起業した会社が問題を抱えるようになったらどのように対応するかペアやグループで意見を述べ合いましょう。

1. What would you do if your start-up company grew too fast and faced some problems?

2. What would you do if your start-up company didn't grow as much as you expected? Would you consider hiring a new CEO for a company you started?

Active Learning **A Unique Company**

興味のある会社を調べ、特にユニークな特徴（採用方法、働く環境、CEO、福利厚生、製品、サービスなど）を見つけ、4つの特徴を4つのスライドに作成してクラスで発表しましょう。

1

2

3

4

THE INTERN

Unit 9

Working Women & Work-Life Balance 仕事と家庭の両立

Background Information

🎧 DL 52 ◎ CD 52

定年退職について読んで、その内容をペアで話し合いましょう。

In the modern world, people have got used to the idea that at a certain age they will stop working and spend the rest of their life in retirement. However, the idea of retiring is a relatively new one, and for most of human history people continued working for as long as they were physically able to. Recently, people have been living for much longer, so the idea that we should stop working in our early sixties and spend thirty years in retirement has started to be challenged. Like Ben Whitaker, more and more people are continuing to work into their seventies, eighties and beyond. As we see in the movie, these people have a lot to offer!

Vocabulary

🎧 DL 53 ◎ CD 53

単語の意味に合う選択肢を選んで記入しましょう（余分な選択肢が２つあります）。

1. relatively　　　　（　　）
2. reflect　　　　　（　　）
3. overcome　　　　（　　）
4. discrimination　　（　　）
5. demanding　　　（　　）

6. expert　　　　　（　　）
7. prejudice　　　　（　　）
8. confess　　　　　（　　）
9. marital　　　　　（　　）
10. infidelity　　　　（　　）

a. 告白する	b. 克服する	c. 偏見	d. 不倫、浮気
e. 課題	f. 反映する	g. 要求の多い	h. 比較的
i. 差別	j. 夫婦の	k. 面倒見のよい	l. 専門家、熟達者

Reading

映画に関する次の文を読みましょう。　　　　DL 54 ~ 57　　CD 54 ~ CD 57

Just as Ben Whitaker is not a typical intern, Jules Ostin is not a typical CEO. As a thirtysomething woman, Jules does not fit people's image of the boss of a major company. While the world is gradually changing, this image is also reflected in reality, as most companies are still run by men, and to get to the top
5　in the business world women need to overcome both discrimination and practical hurdles. As the founder of her own company, Jules has more freedom than many business women to do things her own way. Nevertheless, her life is far from easy.

Before Ben meets Jules he learns from her secretary, Becky, that Jules hates wasting time and can't stand people who talk slowly. At first, this makes her seem
10　like a scary and demanding boss, but it soon becomes clear that Jules is so busy she needs to save every minute she possibly can. Like many women with a lot on their plate, Jules is an expert at multi-tasking, and has no problem writing an email while at the same time talking on the phone. These skills are doubtless key to her success, but this success comes at a price.

15　Due to the demands of her job, it seems impossible for Jules to separate her work and home life, and she doesn't get to spend as much time with her daughter as she would like. We see her working on her computer while she is in bed, and eating pizza at her desk long after her employees have finished work for the day. Fortunately, Jules' husband, Matt, gave up his job in marketing so that he could
20　be a stay-at-home dad, so he is in charge of most of the housework and childcare. Although this arrangement seems to work well for their family, the couple face social prejudice from those around them due to their non-traditional lifestyle.

On a business trip to San Francisco, Jules confesses to Ben that she knows Matt has been cheating on her. Jules is worried that the pressure of their unusual
25　marital roles is the reason for Matt's infidelity, but Ben reassures her that the situation is not her fault. Beyond his role in the company, Jules has now come to depend on Ben as a trusted friend with whom she can share her personal problems and fears.

Reading Comprehension

本文の内容に関して正しい選択肢を選びましょう。

1. Why is Jules not a typical CEO?

   a. Because she has more freedom to control her company than other CEOs.

   b. Because she doesn't need to overcome discrimination and hurdles.

   c. Because male CEOs admire the way she runs her company.

   d. Because she is a female CEO in her thirties.

2. What is Jules good at?

   a. Making demands of people.

   b. Doing several things at the same time.

   c. Encouraging people to talk slowly and clearly.

   d. Doing housework and taking care of children.

3. How does Jules' husband, Matt, support her?

   a. He quits work and takes care of the housework and their child.

   b. He learns about housework from a stay-at-home dad.

   c. He works from home so that he can have more time with Jules.

   d. He changes his lifestyle and tries to overcome prejudice against working women in society.

Expressions

日本語の意味に合うように（　　）内の語句を並べ替えて文を完成させましょう。

1. 顧客の購買パターンに関するデータをあなたに調べてもらいたいのですが。

(data / the / you / on / purchase patterns / to / the / want / over / customer / go)

I _____ .

2. 革靴の配送料金を調べて報告してもらえますか。

(on / report / the / you / and / leather shoes / cost / check / delivery / for)

Can _____ ?

3. たまには定時に退社することを検討すべきです。

(the / a / at / consider / office / should / hour / once in a while / normal / leaving)

You _____ .

MOVIE VIEWING **1** *Listening Comprehension*

🎞 50:18-53:05

JulesとBenが残業をしてオフィスでピザを食べながら話す場面を見て、次の質問に答えましょう。

1. How did another possible CEO describe ATF's e-commerce fashion site?

2. Why did Jules become upset about his remark?

3. How is "legitimate" shortened in the conversation? _____

4. How did Ben respond to her?

5. Where did Ben's office used to be?

6. How does Ben feel about being back in the building he used to work in?

MOVIE VIEWING **2** *Note Taking*

🎞 53:06-56:02

BenがFacebookのアカウントを開設する場面を見て、下線部の情報のメモを取りましょう。

Ben's favorite quote

" _____."

(Who said it first? _____)

Ben's favorite musicians:

- ▪ _____ Cooke

- ▪ Miles _____

- ▪ Billie _____

Ben's favorite books:

- ▪ Books written by (Tom) Clancy

- ▪ Books written by (Robert) Ludlum

- ▪ He is crazy about _____.

Ben's marital status: _____

- ▪ For Facebook, he puts _____.

MOVIE VIEWING 3 Listening Comprehension

▶ 1:00:33-1:03:00

BenがBeckyにアドバイスをする場面を見て、次の質問に答えましょう。

1. Why did Becky become upset and cry after Jules asked Ben to take a look at the customer purchase pattern data first?

2. What degree did Becky get from Penn (University of Pennsylvania)?

   _____ degree

3. How many hours a day does Becky work for Jules? What is Becky's complaint about Jules as a boss?

   _____ hours

4. What advice does Ben give to Becky?

5. What does Becky not want Jules to think of her?

6. What information does Ben give to Becky regarding lack of sleep and weight gain?

MOVIE VIEWING 4 Listening Comprehension

▶ 1:03:01-1:04:14

アメリカの主要都市におけるATF社のオンラインショッピング状況とBenの分析結果に関する場面を見て、次の質問に答えましょう。

1. What does Jules think one of the reasons people are not buying boots is?

2. What does Ben find out about ATF's problems? Fill in the blanks with key words and also choose the appropriate word in the parenthesis.

   - ATF is _____ in the [most / least] expensive place where

     customers are _____ the [most / least].

   - ATF is [most / least] _____ in the channels that have [huge / low]

     _____ in the segments, which appear to have [high / low] value now,

     but in reality, they have the [highest / lowest] spending _____.

Critical Thinking & Discussion

▶ 41:18-46:07

Julesが夫のMattや娘の幼稚園の保護者たちと話すシーンを見て次の質問に答え、働く女性や主夫を選択する男性など、多様な社会における働き方についてペアやグループで意見を述べ合いましょう。

1. [To female students] What would you think of having a stay-at-home spouse?

2. [To male students] What would you think of quitting your job and becoming a house husband / stay-at-home father to support your spouse?

3. Do you think some people are critical of working mothers? If so, why?

4. What kind of support do you think working mothers need at home and in society?

Active Learning Qualities of a Leader

あなたが求めるリーダー像について以下の項目を考え、グループで話し合いましょう。また、自分の持ち合わせている資質と、これから身につける必要のある資質を書いて分析してみましょう。

Qualities I want in a leader (CEO)

-
-
-

Qualities I don't want in a leader (CEO)

-
-
-

Qualities I have now

-
-
-

Qualities I need to develop more

-
-
-

The Possibility of Hiring a New CEO   CEO交代の可能性

©Collection Christophel via AFP

Background Information

DL 58   CD 58

女性の社会進出に関する内容を読んで、日本の状況についてペアで話し合いましょう。

In *The Intern*, Ben, an older, experienced man is happy to work for a younger woman. Similarly, Jules' husband Matt stays at home and takes care of their child while Jules herself works as a high-flying executive. In the world of the movie, it seems traditional gender roles no longer matter and a talented woman can succeed in what used to be considered a man's world. Unfortunately, movies do not always reflect reality: in 2017 only 5% of the largest 500 companies in the USA had a female CEO. And Japan is doing even worse—in 2019 it was ranked 121 out of 153 countries in terms of gender equality. In the real world, it seems we have a long way to go before gender inequality is a thing of the past.

Vocabulary

DL 59   CD 59

単語の意味に合う選択肢を選んで記入しましょう（余分な選択肢が２つあります）。

1. high-flying ( )
2. inequality ( )
3. drive ( )
4. inspire ( )
5. take over ( )
6. hand over ( )
7. oppose ( )
8. victim ( )
9. commitment ( )
10. affair ( )

a. 不平等
b. 鼓舞する
c. 反対する
d. 柔軟性のある
e. 引き渡す、手渡す
f. 献身
g. 引き継ぐ
h. 野心旺盛な
i. 意欲、やる気
j. 手直しする
k. 犠牲
l. 出来事、不倫

Reading

映画に関する次の文を読みましょう。　　　　DL 60 ~ 62　　CD 60 ~ CD 62

　　The success of Jules Ostin's internet startup, About The Fit (ATF), has largely been due to her own drive and ambition. As CEO, Jules has been responsible for overseeing rapid growth in the eighteen months since she founded the company, and her innovative leadership has inspired and motivated her staff. Jules is rightly
5　proud of her abilities and the success she has achieved. Not surprisingly, she is shocked and upset when she learns that the investors in ATF would like to hire an outside professional to take over from her as CEO.

　　When she first hears of the idea from her assistant, Cameron, the thought of handing over control of her company to someone else is enough to bring Jules to
10　tears. But although she strongly opposes the plan, Jules comes to realize that it could perhaps have some advantages. As Cameron points out, in some ways both Jules and ATF have become victims of their own success. Because the company has grown so fast, it is difficult for staff to keep up with orders, with many people working until after midnight. Jules herself regularly complains that she never
15　sleeps, and is so busy that she is late for every meeting she attends. If a new CEO took over some of Jules' day-to-day responsibilities, then she would have more time to focus on the creative side of her job. Jules' family situation also gives her an extra reason to consider accepting a new CEO, as she wonders whether more time at home might be the only way to save her marriage.

20　After looking at several possibilities, Jules interviews Mark Townsend, her first-choice candidate for CEO. After the interview, she explains to Ben that Townsend seems like a good fit for the company and she is planning to offer him the job. However, the following morning Ben tells Jules his true feelings about the situation. He points out that however good a business executive Townsend is,
25　he will never have the same commitment to ATF that Jules does, and that Jules should not feel forced to choose between her career and her marriage. Then, when Matt shows up in her office to confess to his affair and apologize, it seems that Jules finally has the chance to achieve both professional success and personal happiness.

Reading Comprehension

本文の内容に合っているものにはT、合っていないものにはFを記入しましょう。

1. Due to Jules' determination and new ideas and its motivated staff, her company has quickly grown. （　）

2. Jules is not surprised to hear about the possibility of hiring a new CEO to help reduce her workload. （　）

3. Although her initial reaction is different, Jules starts to realize a new CEO may turn around the situation at the company. （　）

4. As Jules' company becomes bigger, both Jules and the employees start to face some problems with overwork. （　）

5. Jules' husband, Matt, feels if Jules spends more time at home, it may save their marriage. （　）

6. Both Jules and Ben think Townsend will be good for ATF. （　）

7. Ben feels it is good for Jules to feel pressured to choose between her career and her family. （　）

Expressions

日本語の意味に合うように空所に適切な語を入れて文を完成させましょう。

1. 彼は私に決断は一晩寝て考えるようにアドバイスしてくれました。

   He _____ me to _____ _____ the decision.

2. 私たちは取引成立を祝して握手を交わしました。

   We _____ _____ on the _____ we agreed on.

3. お邪魔してすみませんが、ベンがどこにいるかご存じですか。

   Sorry to _____, but do you know _____ Ben _____?

4. この件について感傷的になる必要はありません。

   There's no _____ to get all _____ about this _____.

5. あなたのまわりに頼りになる人がいるのを知ることは励みになります。

   It's _____ to know that you have _____ you can count _____ around you.

MOVIE VIEWING ① *Note Taking*

1:43:13-1:44:39

Julesが新しいCEO候補のTownsendに会った後の場面を見て、以下のポイントに注意して
メモを取りましょう。

---

1. What did Townsend say about Jules?

2. What did Townsend say he would like to do with ATF if he became the CEO?

-

-

3. What kind of impression did Jules get about Townsend?

4. What did Jules do after she met and talked with Townsend?

5. What did Townsend tell Jules to do about her decision?

6. What was Jules trying to ask Ben when she said, "You know, if we disagree, he's the tie breaker?"

7. How did Ben respond to Jules' question?

MOVIE VIEWING 2 *Listening Comprehension* ▶ 1:48:28-1:51:10

Townsendと会った翌朝のJulesとBenの会話の場面を見て、次の質問に答えましょう。

1. What does Jules say to Ben about her decision?

2. What did Ben see in Jules when they went to the warehouse together?

3. What does Ben say about Jules' decision to hire a new CEO in order to save her marriage?

4. What is Ben's advice to Jules?

5. Why does Ben think Jules came over to talk to him?

MOVIE VIEWING 3 *Subtitling* ▶ 1:52:09-1:52:32

次の日本語を英語にしましょう。その後で、実際にどのような表現が使われているか場面を見てみましょう。また、ペアを組んでロールプレイをしてみましょう。

マット：	手遅れでないといいけど	_____
	僕のためならやらないで	_____
	正しいと思うことをして	_____
ジュールズ：	会社の経営を続けたいの	_____
	わかってちょうだい	_____
マット：	それなら続けて	_____
	君に不幸になってほしくない	_____

Critical Thinking & Discussion 🎬 1:43:13-1:44:39

CEO候補のTownsendと面接したJulesとBenの会話の場面を見て次の質問に答え、ペアやグループで意見を述べ合いましょう。

1. What do you think you would do if you were Jules? Would you hire Townsend? Explain the reasons.

2. If necessary, what kind of person would you like to hand over your company to? How would you choose that person?

Active Learning : Movie Review

映画 *The Intern* について、各項目をチェック☑しながら評価して星の数を決めた後で、自分なりに批評（映画のよい点や不満な点）を英語で書きましょう。

Rating Criteria	1 ××	2 ×	3 △	4 ○	5 ◎
Plot / Story Development					
Main Cast: Acting / Performance					
Supporting Cast: Acting / Performance					
Scenes / Situations / Setting					
Cinematography / Camerawork					
Script / Language					
Music / Sound Effects					

Movie Review　Stars ☆ ☆ ☆ ☆ ☆

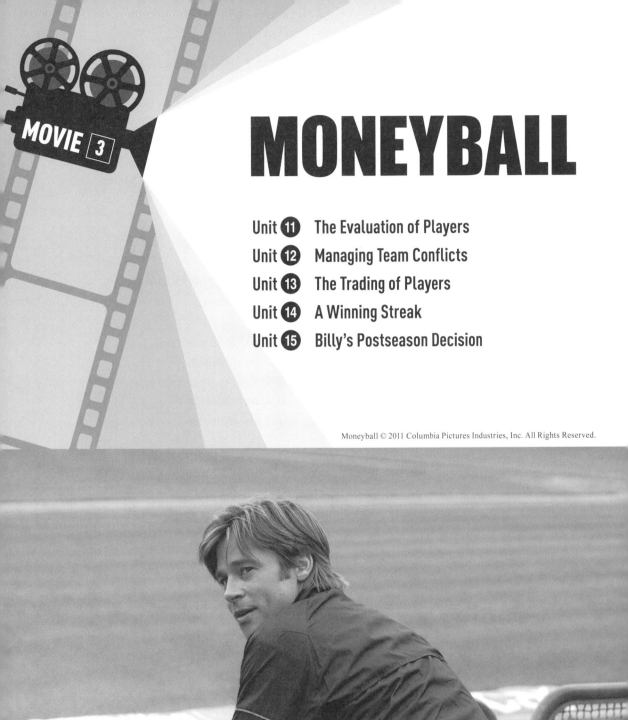

MOVIE 3

MONEYBALL

CAST

Billy Beane   Brad Pitt

General manager of the Oakland Athletics, Major League Baseball team

Peter Brand   Jonah Hill

Billy's assistant general manager

Art Howe   Philip Seymour Hoffman

Manager of the Oakland Athletics

Scott Hatteberg   Chris Pratt

Injured catcher traded to the Athletics

David Justice   Stephen Bishop

Aging outfielder traded to the Athletics

DIRECTED BY
Bennett Miller

■ BRAD PITT ■

1963年、アメリカ・オクラホマ生まれ。91年の『テルマ＆ルイーズ』、翌年の『リバー・ランズ・スルー・イット』で注目を集め、以降人気スターとなる。『ワンス・アポン・ア・タイム・イン・ハリウッド』(19) でアカデミー賞®助演男優賞を受賞。その他の代表作に『セブン』(95)、『12モンキーズ』(95)、『ファイト・クラブ』(99)、『オーシャンズ』シリーズ、『バベル』(06)、『ベンジャミン・バトン 数奇な人生』(08)、『イングロリアス・バスターズ』(09)、『ツリー・オブ・ライフ』(11)、『それでも夜は明ける』(13) などがある。また、02年に映画制作会社「プランBエンターテインメント」を設立し、プロデューサーとして『ディパーテッド』(06)、『それでも夜は明ける』『ムーンライト』(16) でアカデミー賞®作品賞を受賞している。

■ Sabermetrics ■

本作で重要な役割を果たす「セイバーメトリクス」とは、SABR (Society for American Baseball Research：アメリカ野球学会) と metrics (測定基準) を組み合わせた造語で、野球の歴史やデータを専門とする野球ライターのBill Jamesによって提唱された。統計学を用いたデータ分析をチーム経営、選手評価、戦略に活用する手法で、従来は経験に頼っていた野球の世界に革命をもたらした。

Plot Synopsis

 DL 63 CD 63

映画のあらすじを読んで、興味深いと思われる点をペアで話し合いましょう。

These days, sport is big business, and more and more it is the teams with deeper pockets that can expect greater success. Based on a true story, *Moneyball* is about the Oakland Athletics of 2002, a Californian baseball team that bucked this trend to win a record 20 games in a row. Billy Beane (Brad Pitt) is the Athletics' general manager who refuses to have his hands tied by the traditions of baseball and pioneers a new approach to building a successful team. Working alongside Peter Brand, a young assistant, Beane uses statistical analysis to identify players he can pick up at bargain prices and mold into a winning team. Despite the opposition of the coaching staff and a terrible start to the season, Billy and Peter defy the odds to successfully build a play-off team.

Vocabulary

 DL 64 CD 64

単語の意味に合う選択肢を選んで記入しましょう（余分な選択肢が２つあります）。

1. buck	(	)	**6.** odds	(	)
2. statistical	(	)	**7.** lure away	(	)
3. analysis	(	)	**8.** negotiation	(	)
4. identify	(	)	**9.** irrelevant	(	)
5. defy	(	)	**10.** intrigued	(	)

a. 交渉　　　　　　**b.** 無関係な　　　　**c.** 関連する　　　**d.** 識別する、特定する

e. 押し付ける　　　**f.** 逆らう、反対する　**g.** 分析　　　　　**h.** ものともしない、覆す

i. 統計的な　　　　**j.** 勝算、見込み　　　**k.** 引き抜く　　　**l.** 興味をそそられた

Reading

映画に関する次の文を読みましょう。　　　🎧 DL 65 ~ 68　◎ CD 65 ~ ◎ CD 68

　　In 1980, 18-year old Billy Beane faced a huge decision. Academically gifted and an exceptionally talented sportsman, Billy had been offered both a scholarship to a top university and a professional contract with a Major League Baseball team. Although Billy and his parents understood the importance of a good education, the
5　huge signing bonus offered to Billy as a first-round draft pick persuaded them to accept the scouts' offer. Soon afterwards, Billy graduated from high school and began life as a pro ball player.

　　Twenty years later, although Billy's playing career is over, he is still working in baseball and is now general manager (GM) of the Oakland Athletics.
10　But the Athletics are a team with a problem. Despite some good seasons, they are increasingly unable to compete financially with the bigger teams, and in 2001 face a crisis moment when their three star players are lured away by big money offers. Frustrated with his small recruitment budget and the scouts' old-fashioned player evaluation methods, Billy knows something must change if
15　he is to build a successful team.

　　Peter Brand, a young university graduate, is working in a minor role at the Cleveland Indians team. During a failed negotiation to trade players with the Indians, Billy notices Peter's contribution and later seeks him out. A nervous young man with no background in baseball, Peter nevertheless has some
20　revolutionary ideas about how to evaluate and recruit players. Coming to the sport as an outsider, Peter has realized that the way baseball scouts and managers judge players has often been based on irrelevant factors, such as appearance, age, and personality. But baseball is a conservative and traditional sport, and Peter's logical and systematic approach has not been popular with big teams.

25　　Billy, desperate to find a way to compete with the richer teams, is intrigued by Peter's insights. In order to test whether or not Peter's analysis produces an answer Billy agrees with and whether he is brave enough to give that answer, Billy asks Peter if, back in 1980, Billy himself really should have been a first draft pick. Although Peter is reluctant to answer, he admits that he would have only
30　picked Billy in the ninth draft. Impressed with Peter's honesty and his analytical thinking, Billy knows he has found the man to help him rebuild the Oakland Athletics with the money they can afford to spend.

Reading Comprehension

本文の内容に合っているものにはT、合っていないものにはFを記入しましょう。

1. Billy wanted to play baseball professionally after high school, but his parents persuaded him to go to university first. ( )

2. In 2001, the Oakland Athletics had the problem of replacing three main players, who had been taken by richer teams, with their limited budget. ( )

3. As the general manager of the Oakland Athletics, Billy is satisfied with the way his veteran scouts evaluate players for their team. ( )

4. Peter, who used to play baseball at university, currently plays a major role in recruiting and trading players for the Cleveland Indians. ( )

5. Peter disapproves of the fact that scouts and managers often evaluate players based on their appearance and personality, instead of their skills. ( )

6. Baseball is an innovative sport and big teams have adopted the computer-based systematic analysis Peter introduced. ( )

7. When Billy asked Peter about his draft pick 20 years ago, Peter said he would have picked him in the first round without a signing bonus. ( )

 ## Expressions

太字の表現の最も適切な意味を選択肢から選びましょう。

1. Baseball thinking is **medieval**.
   a. refreshing   **b.** outdated   **c.** moderate   **d.** revolutionary

2. I think it's a good thing that you **got him off your payroll**.
   a. hired him   **b.** supported him   **c.** fired him   **d.** paid him

3. We are going to **stand behind** him if he decides to play for us.
   a. adopt   **b.** approve   **c.** persuade   **d.** support

MOVIE VIEWING  **Dictation & Role Play**

▶ 16:43-18:28

会議の後でBillyがPeterに話をする場面を見て空所の部分を書き取り、質問に答えましょう。
その後で、セリフをペアで読む練習をしてからロールプレイをしてみましょう。

Billy: Hey.

Peter: Hello.

Billy: Who are you?

Peter: I'm Peter Brand.

Billy: What do you do?

Peter: I'm ¹_____ Mark Shapiro.

Billy: So, what do you do?

Peter: ²_____ right now.

Billy: Been on the job long? First job in baseball?

Peter: It's ³_____.

Billy: Wow, congrats.

Peter: Thank you.

Billy: First job. ⁴_____? Why does Mark listen to you?

Peter: I don't think ... I don't think he does very often.

Billy: He just did.

Peter: Well, ⁵_____ ... I think he was more listening to Bruce than myself.

Billy: Who are you?

Peter: I'm Peter Brand.

---

1. What is Peter's position?

2. What does Peter do at work?

3. Has Peter worked in the baseball industry or any other business before?

4. Why do you think Billy asked Peter whose nephew he was? What does he imply?

5. Why do you think Billy asks Peter who he is twice?

Listening Comprehension

メジャーリーグのスカウトがBillyと両親に会う場面を見て、次の質問に答えましょう。

1. What qualities does the scout say Billy has?

2. Which major team drafted Billy?

3. What does Billy's mother want him to do?

Which university offered Billy a scholarship?

What does the scout say to her?

4. What does Billy's father say to Billy towards the end of the meeting?

MOVIE VIEWING 3 *Subtitling*

BillyがPeterに自分をドラフトで1巡目に選んだか尋ねる場面を見て、次のセリフの日本語字幕を1行13字以内で作成しましょう。その後で、字幕では実際にどのような表現が使われているか見てみましょう。

English Script	Japanese Subtitle
Billy: Would you have drafted me in the first round?	_____
Peter: I'd have taken you in the ninth round.	_____
No signing bonus.	_____
I imagine you would've passed	_____
and taken that scholarship.	_____
Billy: Yeah.	_____
Pack your bags, Pete.	_____
I just bought you	_____
from the Cleveland Indians.	_____

Critical Thinking & Discussion

26:55- 28:53

Peterの選手評価に対する考えを聞いて次の質問に答え、ペアやグループで意見を述べ合いましょう。

1. What are some of the reasons some players are overlooked?

2. Do you think statistics are the best way to find talented athletes?

3. If you got drafted by an NPB (Nippon Professional Baseball) or MLB (Major League Baseball) team, would you choose to go pro or go to university first?

Active Learning   If You Were a GM ...

あなたは弱小チームのGMで、限られた資金で資金力豊富な強豪チームと戦う必要があります。効果的な戦略と、魅力的なチーム作りのために、福利厚生や賞など選手のモチベーションを高めるためのアイデアをグループで出し合ってクラスで発表しましょう。

Name of the team:

Type of sport:

Team's motto:

Come up with some strategies to play against strong teams.

-
-
-

Come up with some ideas to motivate players on the team.

-
-
-

MONEYBALL

Managing Team Conflicts　チームマネジメントにおける衝突

Movie Review

🎧 DL 69　◎ CD 69

映画の批評を読んで、その内容をペアで話し合いましょう。また、この批評家は映画にいくつ星を付けたか考えてみましょう。

> All sports fans love the story of an underdog, and even more so when it is true. *Moneyball* is one of the great sports movies, telling a simple story and sticking close to the facts. The clever use of authentic baseball footage gives the movie the feel of a documentary, but with the pace of a drama. Brad Pitt is utterly convincing as Oakland Athletics general manager Billy Beane, and the supporting cast, particularly Jonah Hill and Philip Seymour Hoffman, also put in strong performances. The compelling human drama of Beane's struggle to revolutionize baseball management will appeal even to those with no interest in the sport.

Vocabulary

🎧 DL 70　◎ CD 70

単語の意味に合う選択肢を選んで記入しましょう（余分な選択肢が2つあります）。

1. underdog	(　)	**6.** run into	(　)
2. footage	(　)	**7.** afoot	(　)
3. utterly	(　)	**8.** disastrous	(　)
4. compelling	(　)	**9.** grievance	(　)
5. revolutionize	(　)	**10.** criticism	(　)

a. 映像素材	**b.** 出くわす、ぶち当たる	**c.** 人騒がせ	**d.** 批評
e. 無関係の	**f.** 進行中で	**g.** 弱者	**h.** 苦情、腹立ち
i. 人の心をつかむ	**j.** 変革を起こす	**k.** 悲惨な、破滅的な	**l.** 完全に

Reading

映画に関する次の文を読みましょう。　　DL 71 ~ 74　　CD 71 ~　CD 74

After persuading Peter to join him at the Oakland Athletics (A's), Billy takes time to learn more about his young assistant's revolutionary theories. But while Billy himself is convinced that following Peter's advice will lead to success, he runs into fierce opposition from other staff at the A's.

5　　Grady Fuson, the long-serving head scout at the club, strongly disagrees with the idea that you can judge a baseball player by statistics alone, and he and Billy enter into a stand-up argument about the changes afoot at the A's. Grady believes that only long experience and intuition can predict whether a player will be successful, and thinks that listening to Peter will lead to a disastrous season for

10　　the team, and ultimately cost Billy his job. Billy, however, stands firm. He fires Grady and promotes Kubota, a junior scout with little baseball experience, to take his place. The Oakland revolution has begun.

With Grady out of the way, Billy and Peter might think their lives will become a little easier. However, they soon find that the coaching staff are also struggling

15　　with the new system. Against their wishes, Billy had signed three new players that he and Peter believed they could build a team around—David Justice, who is coming to the end of his career, Scott Hatteberg, who has a long-term injury problem, and Jeremy Giambi, who is seen as a troublemaker off the field. While Billy and Peter think these issues are irrelevant, Art Howe, the field manager,

20　　disagrees. He doesn't think the new players are good enough, and refuses to use them in the way that Billy wants. Although Billy insists that the coaches teach Hatteberg, who used to be a catcher, to play in the first base position, Art just doesn't believe that he can do it even with training. Art has already argued with Billy about his contract conditions, and it seems that their working relationship is

25　　breaking down.

Meanwhile, the wider world is becoming aware of the problems at the A's. At the start of the season, journalists bombard the new players with difficult questions, and ex-scout Grady takes to the radio to air his grievances. With public criticism mounting, Billy is coming under increasing pressure for his new team to

30　　produce results on the field.

Reading Comprehension

本文の内容に関して正しい選択肢を選びましょう。

1. What does Grady Fuson say about statistical analysis of baseball players?
   a. You can pretty much evaluate baseball players with statistics.
   b. You need to hold a try-out session for baseball players to see their real ability.
   c. You can't evaluate baseball players using only numbers.
   d. You need to interview baseball players and ask them about their strengths and weaknesses on the field.

2. What do Billy and Peter think about the three players they hired?
   a. They may all have some kind of problems, but they will help build a strong team.
   b. Their problems on and off the field may cause some trouble in the future.
   c. They are young but very talented players and they will fit into the team well.
   d. They will get along well with players and coaches at the A's.

3. What does Art Howe think of using Scott Hatteberg on first base?
   a. He thinks Scott will be a good first baseman if they train him.
   b. He thinks Scott should be a catcher again after he recovers from his injury.
   c. He wants to use Scott at first base, but Scott refuses to accept that idea.
   d. He doesn't think Scott can play as first baseman even if they train him.

Expressions

太字の表現の最も適切な意味を選択肢から選びましょう。

1. **My hat's off to** him.
   a. I will put on my hat for him.   b. My hat will be given to him.
   c. He gave me courage.   d. I respect him.

2. You always **figure** something **out**.
   a. solve   b. remove   c. request   d. prevent

3. They're going to **throw** you **under the bus**.
   a. misunderstand   b. trust   c. sacrifice   d. supervise

MOVIE VIEWING  *Dictation & Shadowing*

🎞 30:07-31:11

監督のArt HoweがBillyに不満を述べる場面を見て空所の部分を書き取り、質問に答えましょう。その後で、役になりきってセリフのシャドーイングをしてみましょう。

Art: Who's the kid?

Billy: A friend of mine.

Art: I can't manage this team under a one-year contract.

Billy: Well, sure you can.

Art: No, I can't.

Billy: Okay. I gotta [1]_____. After that, I'll take a good long look at your contract.

Art: How about you [2]_____, then put a team on the field.

Billy: All right. At this moment, if a grounder's hit to first, nobody's gonna be there to stop it from rolling.

Art: It's not easy doing what I do under the cloud of a one-year contract.

Billy: Okay, I understand that. [3]_____.

Art: I know, I know you have. A one-year contract means the same thing to a manager as it does to a player. [4]_____. Which is strange after a 102-win season.

Billy: I see. If you [5]_____, nobody gives a shit.

Art: So it's on me now?

Billy: No, Art, [6]_____. And the kid is the new assistant GM.

Art: Okay.

---

1. What is Art Howe complaining about?

2. How does Billy respond to Art? What does Billy think he needs to do first?

3. What does Art say about Billy's priority?

4. How did the Oakland Athletics do last season?

5. What does Billy say to Art about their last season?

6. Who does Billy think is responsible for the team?

Listening Comprehension

▶ 46:43-49:34

スカウトの **Grady Fuson** が **Billy** のやり方に意見を述べる場面を見て、次の質問に答えましょう。

1. Why is Grady unhappy?

2. Who is the "Google Boy" Grady is referring to?

3. What does Grady say about baseball?

Baseball is not _____ or _____.

4. According to Grady, what do scouts have that other people do not have?

_____ and _____

5. Why does Grady think Billy is doing what he is doing?

6. What does Billy say about the problems of scouts?

MOVIE VIEWING 3 **Subtitling**

▶ 57:40-57:57

Billy と **Art** が選手起用に関して口論する場面を見て、次のセリフの日本語字幕を1行13字以内で作成しましょう。その後で、字幕では実際にどのような表現が使われているか見てみましょう。

English Script	Japanese Subtitle
Art: What are you trying to say?	_____
Billy: I'm saying it doesn't matter what moves I make	_____
if you don't play the team the way they're designed to be played.	_____
Art: Billy, you're out of your depth.	_____
Billy: Why not Hatteberg at first?	_____
Art: Because he can't play first.	_____
Billy: How do you know?	_____
Art: Not my first baseball game.	_____

Critical Thinking & Discussion

1:00:14-1:02:33

Billyが Peterに GMと選手の関係や、選手を解雇する際のアドバイスを伝えている場面を見て次の質問に答え、ペアやグループで意見を述べ合いましょう。

1. What do you think of the reasons Billy mentions about not developing personal relationships with players? Would you feel the same way as Billy if you were a general manager? Or would you like to develop personal relationships with players?

2. What do you think of Billy's advice to Peter regarding cutting players in a straightforward manner? Do you agree with his advice?

Active Learning **Creating Events for Supporters**

グループで興味のあるスポーツを選び、チケット販売拡大の戦略やファン獲得のための選手とサポーターの交流イベント企画を考え、クラスで発表しましょう。

Sports event (date and venue)
Event for supporters:
Date:
Venue:

Ways to increase supporters / fans	Ways to increase ticket sales

Movie Review

DL 75　CD 75

映画の批評を読んで、その内容をペアで話し合いましょう。また、この批評家は映画にいくつ星を付けたか考えてみましょう。

> Despite being a huge sports fan, I found *Moneyball* to be something of a disappointment. For anyone, like me, who only has a limited understanding of how baseball works, then this film may be confusing and hard to follow. Brad Pitt is at his very best as Billy Beane, but is undermined by the script, especially as the scenes involving Billy's family have no relation to the central plotline and add little to the story. With the exception of Billy, the other characters seem undeveloped, and it is hard to even remember who all the players are, let alone care what happens to them.

Vocabulary

DL 76　CD 76

単語の意味に合う選択肢を選んで記入しましょう（余分な選択肢が２つあります）。

1. disappointment （　　）
2. confusing （　　）
3. undermine （　　）
4. update （　　）
5. radical （　　）

6. pursuit （　　）
7. ruthless （　　）
8. devastating （　　）
9. fury （　　）
10. assert （　　）

a. 最新情報	b. 無情な	c. 失望	d. 痛烈な、破壊的な
e. 追求	f. 許せない	g. 激怒	h. ややこしい
i. 断言する、確立する	j. 台無しにする	k. 切り詰める	l. 根本的な、過激な

Reading

映画に関する次の文を読みましょう。　　　　　　DL 77 ~ 80　　CD 77 ~ 　CD 80

　　Billy Beane hates losing. For a professional sportsman, this is hardly surprising. But Billy *really* hates losing—so much so that he cannot bring himself to watch his own team play, and instead gets Peter to send him score updates by text message. And although the Oakland A's had had a great season in 2001, for
5　Billy, losing the final game made it all meaningless.

　　At the start of the following season, Billy's hopes are high. He has confidence in Peter's analysis, and has managed to recruit the players he wanted. However, the A's get off to a terrible start, losing 14 of 17 games. Media criticism of the radical changes that he and Peter introduced is increasing, and Billy knows
10　that continued failure could leave his job on the line. The owner of the A's, Steve Schott, is also concerned about his team's poor form, and calls Billy and Peter to his office. They manage to persuade Steve that they need more time, and that the results will turn around by July, but Billy still feels under pressure.

　　In his pursuit of victory, Billy needs to be ruthless. As general manager, a key
15　part of his job is recruiting new players for the A's. However, this also means that he is responsible for cutting and trading players. As a former player himself, Billy knows how devastating it can be for a player to be cut from the team, or suddenly traded. Even so, the needs of the team come first, and there is no room for debate or sentiment in Billy's decision making.

20　　To Billy's fury, manager Art Howe goes against his wishes and selects Carlos Peña to play on first base. Then, after the A's lose the game, Billy finds the players, led by Jeremy Giambi, partying in the locker room. For Billy, these two things are unforgivable. In a series of phone calls the following morning, Billy negotiates with other general managers and trades both Peña and Giambi. Although Peter
25　tries to talk him out of it, Billy insists and the two players have no choice but to leave the A's. Billy has asserted his total control over the A's, but now, even more than ever, he needs his team to start winning games.

Reading Comprehension

本文の内容に合っているものにはT、合っていないものにはFを記入しましょう。

1. Billy is nervous about the results of the games, so he doesn't go to the stadium to watch his team play and gets the report from his assistant instead.   (   )

2. Although they recruited new players, the A's do not have a good start to the season and the media starts to criticize Billy's way of managing the team.   (   )

3. Billy and Peter explain to Steve Schott, the owner of the A's, that it will take more time to see the new approach work.   (   )

4. Steve Schott has no doubts about what Billy and Peter are doing and believes that they will produce good results in the end.   (   )

5. As a former baseball player himself, Billy is very sensitive and consults players before cutting and trading them.   (   )

6. Billy is really upset to see players partying in the locker room and taking the loss of the game so lightly.   (   )

7. Peter agrees with Billy about trading Peña and Giambi after seeing their performance on the field.   (   )

Expressions

太字の表現の最も適切な意味を選択肢から選びましょう。

1. Everything is **in a funk**.
   a. ups and downs   **b.** up and running   **c.** uplifting   **d.** down and depressed

2. We're gonna **shake things up**.
   a. reorganize things   **b.** make things up   **c.** reconfirm things   **d.** delete things

3. Do you **project** we'll win more with Hatteberg or Peña at first?
   a. portray   **b.** promise   **c.** pick   **d.** predict

MOVIE VIEWING  *Dictation & Shadowing* ▶ 1:05:29-1:06:25

BillyとPeterがオーナーのSteveにチームの前半戦の状況と今後の見通しを話して説得する場面を見て空所の部分を書き取り、質問に答えましょう。その後で、役になりきってセリフのシャドーイングをしてみましょう。

Billy: Look, Steve. **¹**_____. I believe the record doesn't accurately reflect the strength of this team ... or where we're gonna be at the end of the season. Now, Pete and I here feel very strongly that **²**_____.

Peter: Our sample size has just honestly been too small. It's too ...

Billy: Early. It's still early. Where do we expect to be **³**_____ _____?

Peter: Our goal and our expectation ... is by mid-July **⁴**_____ _____. That would be this working.

Billy: That keeps us in the hunt.

Peter: Exceptionally well.

Steve: By July.

Billy: July.

Steve: And what's gonna **⁵**_____? What are you afraid of?

Billy: **⁶**_____. That's why we're here, Steve. That's why we get up in the morning. That's all we do.

---

1. How does Billy try to convince Steve about the way he's managing the team?

2. What does Billy say to Steve about the team's record after several games of the season?

3. What does Peter say to Steve about the game results so far?

4. What does Peter say about the team's goal by mid-July?

5. What would Steve like to know?

MOVIE VIEWING 2 — *Listening Comprehension*

▶ 1:08:09-1:09:30

Billyと監督のArtが選手の起用に関して口論する場面を見て、次の質問に答えましょう。

1. What does Art say about Peña?

Peña is _____, he's _____.

2. Why does Billy want to use Hatteberg instead of Peña as a first baseman?

3. What does Billy think about Hatteberg's fielding?

4. Does Art agree with Billy's way of choosing players in the lineup?

5. How does Art respond to Billy regarding the way Art manages his team?

6. What do you think of this argument between Billy and Art?

MOVIE VIEWING 3 — *Subtitling*

▶ 1:14:34-1:15:02

選手トレードの話し合いの場面を見て、次のセリフの日本語字幕を1行13字以内で作成しましょう。その後で、字幕では実際にどのような表現が使われているか見てみましょう。

English Script		Japanese Subtitle
Billy:	And Peña's going too.	_____
Peter:	I don't think you should do that.	_____
	I really don't think you should do that.	_____
Billy:	I want Hatteberg in the lineup tonight.	_____
Peter:	Billy, I think you need to take a minute.	_____
	I think you seriously need to just think about what you're doing.	_____
	Because you're upset.	_____
Billy:	Okay. What am I missing?	_____
Peter:	These are hard moves to explain to people.	_____
Billy:	Why is that a problem, Pete?	_____
Peter:	Don't make an emotional decision, Billy.	_____

Critical Thinking & Discussion ▶ 1:13:15-1:20:46

Billyの選手トレードのやり方や、監督に対して選手起用の指示を与える場面を見て次の質問に答え、ペアやグループで意見を述べ合いましょう。

1. What do you think of the way that Billy trades players to shake things up after losing a game?

2. If you were a general manager, would you meddle in the way the manager chooses players for the lineup?

3. Would you have continued to use Peña, an All-Star experienced first baseman, or used Hatteberg, who is new at first but may produce more walks to the first base?

Active Learning Players' Commercial Endorsements

あなたは広告代理店で働いています。ある企業がスポーツ選手を起用して広告を作るように依頼してきました。企業のイメージに合う選手を選び、画像とキャッチフレーズを作成してチラシ用の広告案を作りましょう。

The name of the company	The name of an athlete

The visual image and the tagline for the advertisement

MONEYBALL

Unit 14

A Winning Streak チーム連勝記録

Background Information

 DL 81　CD 81

野球選手とドラフトについて読んで、その内容をペアで話し合いましょう。

> The story of Matt Harrington should be a lesson to us all. As a talented high school pitcher, Harrington was picked in the 2000 Major League Baseball draft. Although he was offered a $4 million contract by the Colorado Rockies, Harrington's agent was not satisfied, and rejected the offer. The following year, after a poor season and having hired a new agent, Harrington was drafted by a different team and this time was offered a contract of just over $1 million, still a tidy sum for most people. Again though, his agent did not think the money was enough. By 2007, having also turned down further offers, Harrington was playing in independent leagues and working other jobs to make ends meet. The lesson? Know your worth and pick your advisors wisely!

Vocabulary

DL 82　CD 82

単語の意味に合う選択肢を選んで記入しましょう（余分な選択肢が２つあります）。

1. reject	( )	**6.** morale	( )
2. tidy	( )	**7.** credit	( )
3. tactics	( )	**8.** reinforce	( )
4. catastrophic	( )	**9.** frantic	( )
5. restore	( )	**10.** consecutive	( )

a. 勇気　　　　**b.** 強化する　　**c.** 戦術　　　　**d.** 功績を認める

e. 士気　　　　**f.** 断る　　　　**g.** 連続した　　**h.** 取り乱した、必死の

i. 壊滅的な　　**j.** 連勝　　　　**k.** かなりの　　**l.** 戻す、修復する

Reading

映画に関する次の文を読みましょう。　　🎧 DL 83 ~ 86　💿 CD 83 ~ 💿 CD 86

In baseball, the role of the general manager is as much about business as sport, with responsibility for hiring players and negotiating contracts. Team selection and tactics are usually left to the field manager. However, after the Oakland A's catastrophic start to the 2002 season, Billy Beane decides he needs
5　to get more directly involved.

Billy and Peter have been using statistical analysis to recruit players, and now they begin to apply these same methods to coaching. By looking at detailed information about individual players, they come up with specific ideas to improve their performance. Not all the players, however, appreciate this approach. Aging
10　star David Justice, playing for his fourth MLB team, doesn't believe Billy's advice applies to him, but Billy manages to convince David to use his experience to help his younger teammates. Another of Billy's new signings, former Boston Red Sox catcher Scott Hatteberg, has been struggling in his new role of first baseman. Manager Art Howe did not want Scott on the team, so Billy delivers a pep-talk to
15　restore his damaged confidence. David, showing the leadership that Billy hoped for, also does his best to boost Scott's morale.

Gradually the season begins to turn around, and soon the team has won seven games in a row. It seems that Billy's efforts with the players have paid off, even though the media are incorrectly crediting Art Howe with inspiring the
20　improvement. But although the wins keep coming, Billy knows he must reinforce the team in order to have a chance of making the play-offs. In a frantic session of trading, Billy and Peter manage to negotiate deals for the players they need to continue the winning streak.

Before long, the A's have recorded their 14th straight win—the most by any
25　major league team that season. Suddenly, despite their bad start, Billy's team are top of the league. Three more wins extend the streak to 17, making it the most consecutive games won by any team since 1953. When the streak reaches 19, the A's need just one victory over the Kansas City Royals to break the all-time record. After some tense moments, Scott Hatteberg, to everybody's surprise, smashes a
30　home run to win the game, and the A's have entered the history books.

Reading Comprehension

本文の内容に関して正しい選択肢を選びましょう。

1. What does the veteran player David Justice think about Billy's advice?
   a. He agrees with Billy and he feels players, young and old, should follow his advice.
   b. He feels advice should come from the field manager, not the general manager.
   c. He feels Billy's advice applies to new players, but not to a veteran player like him.
   d. He feels Billy should show leadership and coach new players since Billy was once a player himself.

2. How do the media react to the Oakland Athletics' consecutive wins after the disastrous start to the season?
   a. The media start to criticize the way Billy manages the team too directly.
   b. The media start to report on the unexpected trading of players in the middle of the season.
   c. The media start to predict the MVP (Most Valuable Player) of the season.
   d. The media start to praise the way the manager, Art Howe, inspires the team.

3. What happened in the game against the Kansas City Royals?
   a. The A's lost the game against the Kansas City Royals.
   b. The A's won the game and made the record winning streak.
   c. A Royals player surprisingly hit a home run in the last inning.
   d. The A's manager refused to use Scott Hatteberg in that game.

 ## Expressions

太字の表現の最も適切な意味を選択肢から選びましょう。

1. He **is adept at** drawing walks.
   a. is poor at   b. is surprised at   c. is pleased at   d. is skilled at

2. The A's have won seven **in a row**.
   a. by a fluke   b. consecutively   c. in the front row   d. for the first time

3. Who am I **getting fleeced** for?
   a. getting overcharged   b. getting paid   c. getting dressed   d. getting hit

MOVIE VIEWING **1** *Dictation & Role Play*

🎬 1:22:18-1:24:20

Billyがベテラン選手のDavidと話す場面を見て空所の部分を書き取り、質問に答えましょう。
その後で、セリフをペアで読む練習をしてからロールプレイをしてみましょう。

Billy: Mr. Justice. Had a few thoughts.

David: Yeah?

Billy: Yeah.

David: Gonna teach me some things?

Billy: Excuse me?

David: Never seen a GM talk to players like that, man.

Billy: You never seen a GM who was a player.

David: Huh.

Billy: We got a problem, David?

David: No, it's okay. [1]_____. It's patter. It's for effect. But it's for them, all right? That shit ain't for me.

Billy: Oh, you're special?

David: You're paying me [2]_____, man, so, yeah … maybe I am, a little bit.

Billy: No, man, I ain't paying you 7. [3]_____. That's what the New York Yankees think of you. They're paying you [4]_____ to play against them.

David: [5]_____, Billy?

Billy: David, you're 37. How about you and I be honest about what each of us want out of this? I wanna milk the last ounce of baseball you got in you. And you wanna [6]_____. Let's do that. I'm not paying you for the player [7]_____. I'm paying you for the player you are right now. You're smart. You get what we're trying to do here. [8]_____. Be a leader. Can you do that?

David: All right. I got you.

Billy: We're cool?

David: We're cool.

---

1. Why does David think he is special?

2. How much are the New York Yankees paying for David?

3. What is Billy trying to say to David?

MOVIE VIEWING  *Listening Comprehension*

🎬 1:25:10-1:26:18

Billyと Peterが選手にプレーについてアドバイスをする場面を見て、次の質問に答えましょう。

1. What advice does Billy give to Hatteberg?

2. What does Hatteberg notice after he looks at some data with Peter?

3. According to Billy, what do players need to do to win?

4. What does Billy tell players not to do?

5. What does Billy tell players to do if a player on another team bunts on them?

6. What advice does Billy give about stealing?

MOVIE VIEWING  *Subtitling*

🎬 1:34:39-1:35:54

選手に戦力外通知をする場面を見て、次のセリフの日本語字幕を1行13字以内で作成しましょう。その後で、字幕では実際にどのような表現が使われているか見てみましょう。

English Script	Japanese Subtitle
Billy: Mags.	_____
Mike: Hey, Billy.	_____
I know I've been struggling lately.	_____
But the second half of the season, definitely turn it around.	_____
Billy: Mike, I need you to stop getting dressed.	_____
Mike: Traded?	_____
Billy: I'm sorry for the crap news.	_____
I know it hurts.	_____
Mike, I can't have 26 guys in the clubhouse.	_____
Mike: I get it. I get it.	_____
Billy: Okay. Thanks.	_____

Critical Thinking & Discussion

1:45:58-1:51:19

シーズン後半における連勝中の監督の選手起用や、Billyがチームで本当にやりたいことを語る場面を見て次の質問に答え、ペアやグループで意見を述べ合いましょう。

1. Billy says winning the ALDS (American League Division Series) doesn't mean anything. Why do you think he says that?

2. What does Billy really want to do?

3. If you were a general manager, what do you think your motivations would be?

Active Learning A.I. vs. Human Beings

A.I.の発達により、機械が人間にとって代わると予想される仕事と、人間にしかできないと思われる仕事を調べてリストにしましょう。また、これからの時代に必要な知識やスキル、人間らしい生き方について話し合いましょう。

Things A.I. is good at	Things humans are good at

Skills people need to develop in the 21st century

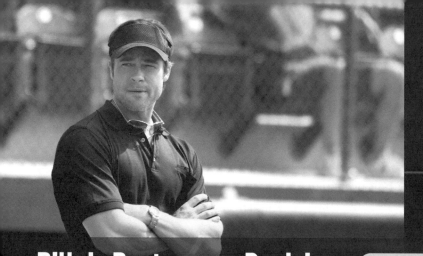

MONEYBALL

Billy's Postseason Decision
シーズン終了後のビリーの決断

Background Information

DL 87　CD 87

実話を映画化する際の問題点について読んで、その内容をペアで話し合いましょう。

> Making a movie based on a real life story can pose special challenges for scriptwriters and directors. While a documentary must stick to the facts, and a fictional drama offers more creative license, filmmakers must tread a fine line when portraying real people in a dramatization of a true story. In *Moneyball*, the manager of the A's, Art Howe, played by Philip Seymour Hoffman, comes across as old-fashioned and ineffective, and causes many problems for Billy Beane. However, after seeing his character on screen, the real-life Art was not happy with how he appeared in the movie. It seems that when real people are involved, both filmmakers and filmgoers should try to distinguish fact from fiction.

Vocabulary

DL 88　CD 88

単語の意味に合う選択肢を選んで記入しましょう（余分な選択肢が２つあります）。

1. tread	( )	**6.** magnitude	( )
2. ineffective	( )	**7.** haunted	( )
3. distinguish	( )	**8.** perspective	( )
4. defeat	( )	**9.** resounding	( )
5. intensify	( )	**10.** determination	( )

a. 効果のない、無能な	**b.** とりつかれた	**c.** 開拓する	**d.** 考え方、見方
e. 決断力、決意	**f.** 負け、敗北	**g.** 大きさ	**h.** 強くなる、激しくなる
i. 印象づける	**j.** 区別する	**k.** 進む、歩む	**l.** 圧倒的な、目覚ましい

Reading

映画に関する次の文を読みましょう。　　🎧 DL 89 ~ 92　◉ CD 89 ~ ◉ CD 92

　　After their poor start to the season, the Oakland Athletics' record-breaking 20 game winning streak has propelled the team into the play-offs for the second consecutive year. But Billy knows that what matters is not winning the American League Division Series (ALDS)* or American League Champion Series (ALCS)**.
5　For his new methods to change the way baseball operates, he feels that nothing less than a World Series win will do. Unfortunately, it is not to be. The A's lose to the Minnesota Twins in the ALDS, and their season ends in defeat. Moreover, criticisms of Billy and Peter's statistical revolution intensifies. For Billy, whose dream was to change baseball, this was almost as bad as the loss itself.

10　But while the doubters remain, other influential people within the sport are impressed with what Billy's cut-price team has achieved. The Boston Red Sox are one of the oldest and biggest clubs in baseball, and their owner, John Henry, invites Billy to Fenway Park, the home of the Red Sox, to make him an offer. John wants Billy to manage the club, and with an offer of $12,500,000 is willing
15　to make him the highest paid general manager ever in the sport.

　　Billy, while tempted by the Red Sox's offer, is still devastated by the play-off defeat. With his hatred of losing, Billy finds it hard to realize the magnitude of what he has achieved at Oakland that season. Moreover, he is haunted by memories of his high school decision, when he chose the riches of pro baseball over a university
20　scholarship, only for his playing career to fizzle out in disappointment. However, a conversation with Peter changes Billy's perspective, and helps him to understand that, despite losing the play-off, their season has nevertheless been a resounding success.

　　Ultimately, Billy decides to turn down John's offer in order to stay in California
25　close to his daughter. He remained the GM at the A's until 2016, and although the A's reached the play-offs again, they never won the World Series. However, in 2004, using the recruitment model pioneered by Billy and Peter, the Boston Red Sox won their first World Series since 1918. Since then, many other teams have emulated Billy's approach, and his analytical methods have now become standard. Billy
30　Beane may not have won the World Series, but there is no doubt that his vision and determination changed baseball.

American League Division Series (ALDS): アメリカンリーグ地区シリーズ
American League Championship Series (ALCS): アメリカンリーグ優勝決定シリーズ

Reading Comprehension

本文の内容に合っているものにはT、合っていないものにはFを記入しましょう。

1. Billy's new approach to managing the team led the A's to play in the play-offs for the first time in the team's history. ( )

2. Criticism of Billy and Peter increased after the A's lost to the Minnesota Twins in the play-offs and did not advance to the World Series. ( )

3. Billy's ultimate goal was to help the A's win the World Series and change the way baseball operates. ( )

4. Despite the media criticism, the owner of the Boston Red Sox evaluates Billy's management style highly and invites him to the ballpark in Boston. ( )

5. If Billy had taken the offer from the Boston Red Sox, he would have been the highest paid general manager in baseball history. ( )

6. Billy does not regret his decision to become a pro baseball player right after high school because he was able to make money. ( )

7. Adopting Billy's analytical approach to baseball helped the Boston Red Sox win the World Series for the first time in many decades. ( )

Expressions

太字の表現の最も適切な意味を選択肢から選びましょう。

1. You know, why someone took so long to hire that guy is **beyond me**.
   a. easy to imagine
   b. beyond recognition
   c. hard to understand
   d. within my reach

2. I don't **get over** these things.
   a. recover from   b. put up with   c. do away with   d. stay away from

3. I know you've got to **let it go**.
   a. keep in touch with it
   b. put it behind you
   c. take good care of it
   d. keep an eye on it

MOVIE VIEWING 1 — *Dictation & Shadowing*

アメリカンリーグ地区優勝決定戦の実況場面を見て空所の部分を書き取り、質問に答えましょう。その後で、アナウンサーや解説者になりきってシャドーイングをしてみましょう。

⚾ American League Division Series (ALDS)   📽 1:51:20-1:51:52

Announcer 1: So, the Oakland A's, going to **1**_____ with the West Division title under their belt.

Announcer 2: Forgive the A's **2**_____ just yet. They have been here before … last year in fact when Oakland went up two games to none on the Yanks in the ALDS … and went nowhere **3**_____ _____. But with a win today over the Twins, Oakland moves into the ALCS for the first time **4**_____.

Commentator 1: But John, remember one thing. Percentages hold up over the course of a season, but for one game, one at bat … throw the percentages out the window.

⚾ After the ALDS play-off series   📽 1:52:24-1:53:07

Commentator 2: What the Minnesota Twins exposed is the fact that the Oakland A's were fundamentally **5**_____. I mean they had **6**_____ that started with the general manager and the brain trust over there thinking they could reinvent baseball. **7**_____ _____ from a statistical, bean-counting point of view. It's won on the field with fundamental play. You have to **8**_____, you have to **9**_____, you have to **10**_____. You gotta get men **11**_____ _____, and you gotta bring them in. And you don't do that with a bunch of statistical gimmicks. **12**_____.

---

1. What happened when the A's went to the play-offs with the Yankees in the previous year?

2. When was the last time the A's played in the ALCS?

3. What was the result of the play-offs this time?

4. What does Commentator 2 say about the A's after the play-offs?

5. According to Commentator 2, how should baseball be played?

6. Do you agree with what Commentator 2 says about baseball? How do you think baseball should be played?

MOVIE VIEWING  *Listening Comprehension*

🎬 1:54:11-1:58:39

Billyが **Boston Red Sox** を訪れてオーナーの **John Henry** と会談する場面を見て、次の質問に答えましょう。

1. Is Steve, the owner of the Oakland Athletics, renewing Billy's contract?

2. Why did Billy decide to visit the Boston Red Sox?
   - Because it's _____.
   - Because he believes _____ the Curse of the Bambino.
   - Because he hears the Red Sox _____.

3. Who is Bambino? Research some information regarding the Curse of the Bambino.

4. Why does John praise Billy? How much did the Yankees spend per win? How about the Athletics?
   Yankees: _____   Athletics: _____

5. What does John think Billy's method means to other organizations?

6. What does John say about the teams that are not using Billy's method?

7. What does John offer to Billy?

MOVIE VIEWING  *Subtitling*

🎬 2:01:07-2:01:42

Billyが **Peter** にチームで成し遂げたかったことを話す場面を見て、次のセリフの日本語字幕を1行13字以内で作成しましょう。その後で、字幕では実際にどのような表現が使われているか見てみましょう。

English Script	Japanese Subtitle
Billy: I really wanted to win here. I really did.	_____ _____
Peter: I think you won pretty big, Billy.	_____
Billy: Pete, we lost. We lost.	_____
Peter: It's only been a few days. You have to give yourself some time to get over it.	_____
Billy: Man, I don't get over these things. Ever.	_____

Critical Thinking ⊜ Discussion

📽 1:54:54-2:01:00

BillyとBoston Red SoxのオーナーJohnとの話し合いと、Billyがオークランドに帰って
Peterと話す場面を見て次の質問に答え、ペアやグループで意見を述べ合いましょう。

1. What kind of small talk do you think is appropriate in business situations?

2. What qualities do you think general managers should have?

3. Would you have taken the job offer at the Boston Red Sox if you were Billy? What
are some of the important factors when choosing a career?

Active Learning　Movie Review

映画*Moneyball*について、各項目をチェック☑しながら評価して星の数を決めた後で、自分
なりに批評（映画のよい点や不満な点）を英語で書きましょう。

Rating Criteria	1 ××	2 ×	3 △	4 ○	5 ◎
Plot / Story Development					
Main Cast: Acting / Performance					
Supporting Cast: Acting / Performance					
Scenes / Situations / Setting					
Cinematography / Camerawork					
Script / Language					
Music / Sound Effects					

Movie Review　Stars ☆ ☆ ☆ ☆ ☆

本書には CD（別売）があります

Active English through Movies

アクティブ・ラーニング型　映画で学ぶ英語 4 技能

2021 年 1 月 20 日　初版第 1 刷発行
2024 年 2 月 20 日　初版第 7 刷発行

著　者　　塩 見 佳 代 子
　　　　　Matthew Coomber
　　　　　宮 林 賀 奈 子

発行者　　福 岡 正 人
発行所　　株式会社　金 星 堂

（〒 101-0051）東京都千代田区神田神保町 3-21
Tel. (03) 3263-3828（営業部）
(03) 3263-3997（編集部）
Fax (03) 3263-0716
https://www.kinsei-do.co.jp

編集担当　今門貴浩　　　　　　　　　　Printed in Japan
印刷所・製本所／株式会社カシヨ
ISBN978-4-7647-4125-6　C1082